ROLLS-ROYCE V8s

THE MODERN ERA

MICHAEL I. F. PELL
10, The Avenue
Hipperholme
HALIFAX
W. Yorkshire HX3 8NP.

Telephone (0422) 201133

ROLLS-ROYCE V8s

THE MODERN ERA

Ian Adcock

OSPREY
AUTOMOTIVE

First published in Great Britain in 1994
by Osprey, an imprint of Reed Consumer
Books Limited, Michelin House,
81 Fulham Road, London SW3 6RB and
Auckland, Melbourne, Singapore and Toronto

ISBN 1 85532 423 7

Editor Shaun Barrington
Page design Paul Kime/Ward Peacock
Partnership
Printed in Hong Kong
Produced by Mandarin Offset

All photographs courtesy of Rolls-Royce
Motors unless otherwise stated.

With grateful thanks to all those at Crewe who
helped in the preparation of this book.

Half title page
*Special wheel trims round off the
Anniversary Corniche*

Title page
*As a special touch to celebrate 75 years
of Rolls-Royce, the R-R badge was
painted red instead of its usual, more
sombre black on a special export version*

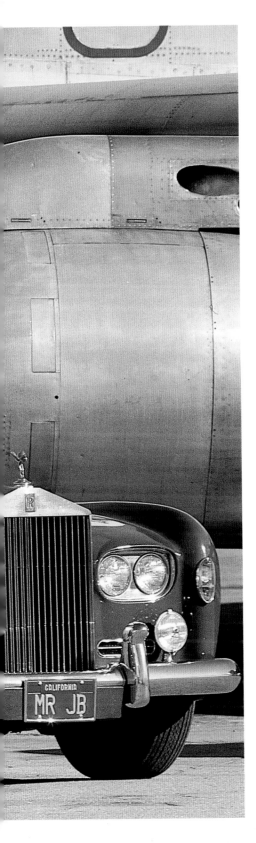

Contents

Introduction

Experts will debate endlessly as to whether Rolls-Royce make, or ever did build, 'the best car in the world' but, few can argue that the Pantheon grille topped by the Spirit of Ecstasy or the interlinked Rs are the most famous automotive symbols in the world. Charles Stewart Rolls' (1877-1910), and Frederick Henry Royces' (1863-1933), families represent the opposite ends of late Victorian society: Rolls was the third son of John Allan Rolls, later Lord Llangattock, and educated at Eton and Cambridge. Royce was one of five children born to James and Mary Royce, impoverished millers from near Peterborough. A few years after moving to London in search of work, Royce's father died and at the age of 10 the young Royce found himself selling newspapers to augment the family income.

Determined to better himself, and with the aid of a generous aunt, Royce got an engineering apprenticeship with the Great Northern Railway. Unable to keep up payments for his apprenticeship, Royce moved to work for a machine tool maker in Leeds in 1880 and then on to jobs with pioneering electrical companies in London and Liverpool. By 1884 Royce had teamed up with Ernest Claremont to establish F H Royce and Company in Manchester manufacturing lamp holders, bells and dynamos. There was nothing innovative about these products, except their refinement and Royce's obsession with perfection, both hallmarks of the cars which later bore his name.

Rolls, meanwhile, was being groomed for the life of ease and luxury a young Baronet could expect at the turn of the last Century. Like Royce, he was a natural mechanic and earned a degree in Mechanical Engineering and Applied Sciences from Cambridge. While there he also bought a 3 3/4 hp Peugeot, his first car and the first seen at the University. By 1903 Rolls was one of the countries' leading motorists and even held the land speed record for a while after driving an 80 hp Mors at 93 mph at Phoenix Park, Dublin. A year earlier Royce had bought his first car, a De Dion Quadricycle which was quickly followed by a Decauville. The fastidious Royce disliked both vehicles immensely and considered them crudely designed and built and despaired at their lack of reliability, especially the electrics which particularly offended him.

In 1903, aided by a mechanic and two apprentices, Royce set about building his own car and on 1 April 1904 Royce drove the first two-cylinder 10 hp car bearing his name out of the Cooke Street factory.

Charles Stewart Rolls, 1877-1910, scion of the Earl of Llangattock had a privileged upbringing typical of the late Victorian landed gentry. He died in tragic circumstances when his Wright biplane crashed

Frederick Henry Royce's background couldn't have been more different from his partners. The son of an impoverished miller, Royce went on to found one of world's greatest engineering concerns. His fanatical pursuit of excellence is still the hallmark of the cars which bear his name

Meanwhile Rolls' passion for motoring had led him in 1902 to establishing C S Rolls and Company as purveyors of prestigious continental marques. But what young Rolls really dreamed of was selling a British car that was at least equal to, if not better than, the European products he sold. In the infant days of the British motor industry virtually everyone knew or had heard of each other. It was a relatively small coterie of enthusiasts and, fortunately, for Rolls and Royce they had a common link. Henry Edmunds, a shareholder in what was by then Royce Ltd, told his friend, the Hon C S Rolls about Manchester's latest car. Not only that, but he persuaded Rolls to meet Royce for lunch at the Midland Hotel, Manchester on Wednesday, 4th May, just five weeks after Royce's first drive in his 10 hp. Despite their utterly different backgrounds, the two immediately hit it off – Rolls later said of Royce that he 'was the man I have been looking for for years' – and after Rolls had driven the car he promptly signed a deal to sell all of Royces' cars from his London showroom. What is more the cars were to be known as 'Rolls-Royce', though that name didn't become official until 23rd December. The World's most famous motoring marque had been born, although Rolls-Royce Ltd didn't officially come into being until 15 March 1906.

No history of the early years of Rolls-Royce would be complete without mentioning Claude Johnson. Often known as the 'hyphen' in Rolls-Royce, Johnson had left his previous job as secretary of what is now the RAC in 1902 and joined C S Rolls. In the ensuing years Johnson played an increasingly important managerial role in the embryonic company, especially after Rolls' death and Royce's breakdown in health shortly afterwards. It was Johnson, in fact, who created the most famous Rolls-Royce of all, 'the Silver Ghost' in 1908 as a publicity exercise. In the same year, Rolls-Royce moved from its cramped Cooke Street premises to a new factory in Nightingale Road, Derby where cars were built until World War 2. Unfortunately Rolls didn't live long enough to savour the fame that the cars would bring, as on 12 July 1910 he was killed in an aircrash at Bournemouth. As well as his name living forever on cars and aero engines around the world, Rolls is, sadly, remembered as Britain's first flying fatality. Royce outlived his young partner for another 23 years, maintaining an iron grip on the Company and its products even though ill health forced him to live in the South of France for much of his later life.

As elegant as the Pantheon grille is, it would look incomplete without the 'Spirit of Ecstasy' adorning it. The statuette was Claude Johnson's idea to prevent owners putting unseemly mascots on the Rolls-Royce radiator. The work of artist Charles Sykes, he reputedly used Eleanor Thornton, secretary to Lord Montagu of Beaulieu, as his model. Although commissioned in 1911 it didn't become a popular fitting until after World War 1.

The years 1914-18 saw Rolls-Royce turn its hand to aero-engine production while armoured cars based on the 40/50 hp chassis – the same as the Silver Ghost's – saw sterling service on battlefields across Europe, Africa and the Middle East.

So successful were Rolls-Royce aero-engines during the conflict, that in peacetime they became the principal profit earner for the group with cars taking second place. Nevertheless, during that time Rolls-Royces' reputation as the world's premier car builders was firmly established. Along the way a factory was opened in Springfield, Massachusetts in 1921 to manufacture chassis there, but only 2990 were built and after a dozen years the operation closed. Despite this hiccough, Rolls-Royce cars thrived and a steady stream of class-leading products such as the 20 hp 'baby Rolls-Royce', the Phantoms I and II, the 20/25 hp, the Wraith and the advanced Phantom III with its 7340 cc V12 engine were much sort after by the rich and famous all over the world. And, while other marques such as Bugatti, Hispano-Suiza or Packard quickly bloomed and died or were taken over and diluted, Rolls-Royce remained independent and aloof.

The post-World War 2 years brought a new way of thinking, the old traditions of coachbuilding were rapidly dying out as mass-production took over. Which meant, of course, that Rolls-Royce had to change with the times as well. Rolls-Royce car production resumed in 1949 at Crewe – where a greenfield site had been chosen immediately before the war as the location for a new factory to produce Merlin aero-engines – with the Silver Wraith which was still offered with coachbuilt bodies. The Phantom IV appeared in 1950 and the UK specification Silver Dawn debuted in 1953, four years after it became Rolls-Royce's first export model. The Dawn is significant in that it was the first common bodyshell for both Rolls-Royce and Bentley apart, that is, from badging and radiators.

The Silver Cloud appeared in 1955, powered by the last in-line six-cylinder Rolls-Royce built and the first to be fitted with an automatic transmission. More significantly for the likes of Freestone & Webb, Hoopers, James Young, Park Ward and H J Mulliner it was the last Rolls-Royce – apart from Phantoms – to have a separate box chassis. It signalled the end of a coachbuilding tradition dating back to beyond the first Rolls-Royce ever built.

As the ensuing chapters will show, Rolls-Royce has had a turbulent time over the past 35 years. The euphoria of glorious 'highs' has been dashed by depressing lows such as the one the company experienced in 1992-93. Shortly before this book was started, savage redundancies had cut the workforce by nearly 50 per cent to just over 1500 workers as a result of the global slump in new car sales. With short time working and

Above
Each Rolls-Royce grille is handmade by skilled craftsmen who stamp their initials on the finished radiator

Right
The most famous radiator in the world? It might look like an assembly of flat surfaces but, in fact, each one is slightly bowed as a perfectly flat surface looks concave. The Greeks called this deliberate geometric distortion 'entasis' and built it into the Parthenon

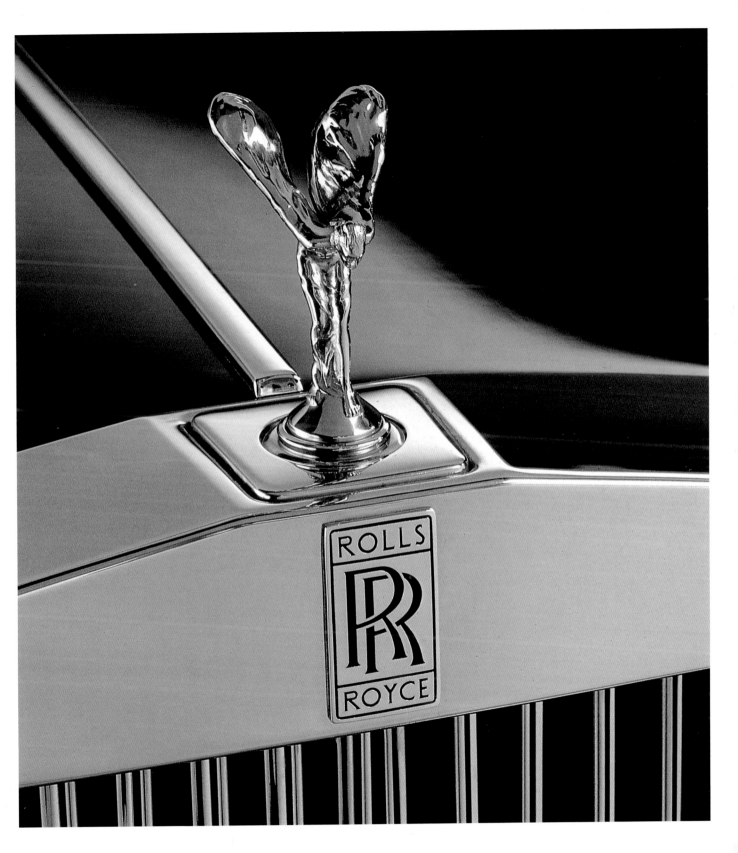

Above

Traditional skills and materials are Rolls-Royce core values. Other manufacturers might be more technically advanced, but none can equal Rolls-Royce when it comes to using wood and leather

machinery standing idle, the Crewe factory at the end of 1992 had a disconsolate air to it. Even so, Sir Henry's motto 'Whatsoever is rightly done, however humble, is noble' is still the guiding philosophy of the remaining workforce, which continues a tradition in perfection 60 years after Frederick Henry Royce died.

Right

Claude Johnson commissioned the 'Spirit of Ecstasy' from Charles Sykes in 1911 to prevent Rolls-Royce owners from using inappropriate mascots on their cars. But, the famous statuette didn't come into regular use by Rolls-Royce until after the World War I

V8 Story

Despite experience and expertise stretching back to World War 1 Rolls-Royce had never been enamoured with Vee-engines for its cars. It was a different story altogether when it came to aero-engines, where the V12 Eagle during the WW1 and, most famously, the Merlin during WW2 established Rolls-Royce as one of the world's leading aero-engine designers and manufacturers.

The first Rolls-Royce V8 was actually inspired by Claude Johnson as early as 1905 in what was quaintly named the 'Invisible Model'. In those far-off times electric cars were still very much in vogue and Johnson decided that Rolls-Royce should build a car which looked like an electric brougham. To achieve a flat deck, Royce designed a wide-angled 3.5-litre V8 which could be located beneath the vehicles' floorboards. But that and the 'Legalimit' variant – so called because Sir Alfred Harmsworth (later Lord Northcliffe), founder of the *Daily Mail* suggested its maximum velocity should be restricted to the country's 20 mph legal speed limit – was a sales failure and only three were built.

It was 30 years before another Vee-engined Rolls-Royce was launched and, although it falls outside the era covered by this book it cannot be ignored as the car in which it was installed, the Phantom III, was, arguably, the final 'no expenses spared' Rolls-Royce built and, more importantly, it was the last car in which Sir Henry (he was knighted in 1930), was involved. It was almost a question of pride which forced Rolls-Royce into building the Phantom III as all of its great rivals – America's Cadillac, Lincoln and Packard and Hispano-Suiza from Spain – all boasted V12 power units for their top-line prestige models. Design work on the Phantom III began in 1932 and despite rapidly failing health Royce continued to work on the project from his bed in the West Wittering house he had used as a summer base since 1917, the winter months being spent at Le Canadel in the South of France. As the months crept by, Royce became increasingly convinced that he would never live to see the Phantom III become a reality sadly his prognosis was correct. At 7 am on 22 April 1933, Sir Frederick Henry Royce – described by Charles Rolls as 'the greatest motor engineer in the world' – passed

The Silver Cloud II was the first Rolls-Royce to have a V8 since the short-lived 'Legalimit' of 1905 with its almost flat vee engine

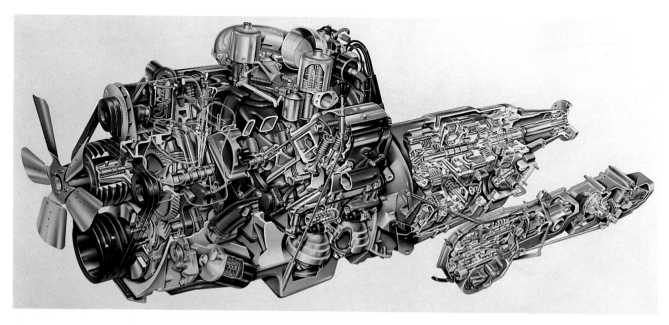

away, two-and-half years before the Phantom III was unveiled.

Royce's place at the head of the Phantom's design team was taken by A G Elliott who had worked with the great man during WWI. The car and engine he produced are a fine testimony to one of the world's premier automobile engineers – not, perhaps, in terms of innovation, but certainly as a perfectionist with an exacting eye for detail. The huge 7338 cc V12 Elliott designed was more a homage to mechanical refinement and excellence than practicality, but it can be argued that if you could afford a Phantom III then you paid someone else to worry about its serviceability. Cylinder head and block – with wet liners – were manufactured from Hiduminium, an aluminium alloy developed by Rolls-Royce for aero engines which, unfortunately, suffered from corrosion problems in service. A gear-driven central camshaft operated the overhead valves via pushrods. Development problems lead to a complete redesign of the cylinder head – although this didn't come into service until 1938, three years after the first car was delivered – and a switch from a quartet of carbs to a single downdraught Stromberg meant the revised cylinder head had four inlet ports instead of the original's half dozen. Nevertheless, output was increased from 189 to 207 bhp. The Phantom III remained in production until 1939 and its demise coincided with the end of an era not only for Rolls-Royce, but also for the world as mankind plunged into its second global conflict within a generation.

In 1946 Rolls-Royce resumed car production, but not at Nightingale Road. Instead, the management decided to utilise the Pyms Lane site at

An early Shadow engine and gearbox assembly. Even before the days when strict exhaust emissions were being demanded the Crewe V8 was a complex piece of engineering

Crewe – which had been built in 1939 to manufacture the Merlin – and concentrate its aero-engine production in Derby. By 1950 Rolls-Royce senior management, headed by technical director, Harry Grylls had decided that the 4.2-litre B60 straight-six – which dated back to 1938 – was rapidly reaching the end of its potential. A new, modern power unit was called for, but what? There already existed the B80, a 5.7-litre straight-eight used to power the Phantom IV, but its length and weight, 700 lbs, mitigated against it being used in future generations of Rolls-Royce cars. A V12 was briefly contemplated, but its size, weight and complexity – combined with the growing popularity of large capacity V8s in the USA – convinced Grylls and his team that eight cylinders were enough. Work began on 5.2- and 5.4-litre engines in the early fifties, but once the first prototype engines had been tested in 1953 it immediately became apparent that if the new engine was to have significant power and torque increases over the B80 then its capacity would need increasing to 6.25 litres. But it was to take another six years before the new 90 deg V8 power unit was unveiled proving that Rolls-Royce's quest for perfection, like 'the march of the human mind', is slow.

It would be reasonable to expect that after such a lengthy gestation the new engine would be a paragon of virtue, but it wasn't. Even the usually deferential *Autocar* of 1960 criticised the new power unit when it

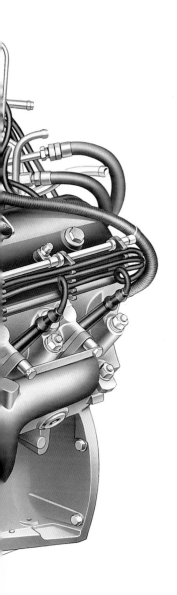

tested the Silver Cloud II on the grounds 'that, even when the engine had reached normal running temperatures, its idling was neither completely smooth nor silent', and that 'it tended to run rather hot when the car was held up in dense city traffic, and would occasionally stall'. Despite its additional two cylinders and 27.5 per cent increase in swept volume over the B60, the new 6.25-litre was 30 lbs lighter thanks to its cast alloy block and cylinder heads. There was nothing revolutionary about the oversquare – 104.1 mm bore/91.4 mm stroke – engine which featured a conventional five-bearing crankshaft and a gear-driven single camshaft in the centre of the Vee. The overhead valves were operated by self-adjusting hydraulic tappets. The firing order was 1R, 1L, 4R, 4L, 2L, 3R, 3L, 2R etc; and the compression ratio was 8:1. Twin inward-facing 1.75 ins SU horizontal carburetters fed a complex double inlet system with each carb feeding cylinders one and four of one bank and two and three of the opposite. The exhaust ports faced outwards and were above the spark plugs, which meant that access to those on the right was via an inspection panel on the inner wheelarch. While plugs on the left could just about be reached from above, that is if the engine wasn't hot. Belt drives at the front of the engine ran the water pump and power steering pump, dynamo and – if fitted – the freon compressor for the airconditioning system.

Rolls-Royce has always been coy about its engines' power outputs, euphemistically referring to them as 'adequate'. But in its description of the new engine *Motor* guesstimated that the V8 produced 325 lb-ft torque and 'must comfortably exceed a genuine 200 bhp'. The first car to receive the new V8 was the Silver Cloud II and the engine remained virtually unchanged for a number of years. In 1962 the Cloud III appeared with the compression ratio raised to 9.0:1 – except for certain export markets which retained the original setting – twin 2 ins SU HD8 carburetters replacing the smaller originals and a nitride hardened crankshaft with larger diameter gudgeon pins installed to cope with the claimed seven per cent power increase. It wasn't until the new, monocoque-bodied Silver Shadow appeared in 1965 that the V8 got its first major revision when new cylinder head castings, with different combustion chamber shape and porting, were fitted. This, together with redesigned exhaust manifolds, allowed the engineers to relocate the spark plugs above the manifolds instead of below as in the past, which must have been a Godsend to thousands of mechanics around the world.

During the next five years the engine received minor improvements such as a viscous cooling fan in 1968, swing-needle SU carburetters,

Fuel injection arrives at last. Nowadays all Rolls-Royce engines are designed to meet the world's strictest emission laws, irrespective of where the car is sold

stainless steel exhaust system and an alternator as standard the following year. All minor cosmetic improvements, but the car's ever increasing weight and stricter exhaust emission regulations – especially from the USA – meant that maintaining the car's performance could only be achieved by increasing engine power. Thus, in 1970 the 6.75-litre V8 was introduced. The additional 520 cc was achieved by installing a new, long-throw crank, con-rods and pistons which increased the stroke from the original's 91.4 mm to 99.1 mm. While 6.75-litres seems plenty big enough these days, Rolls-Royce did experiment with 7.25-litre engines for a while, but wisely decided that increasing concerns over fuel consumption and emission levels would only worsen and, therefore, abandoned the project. As in the past, Rolls-Royce remained suitably shy about revealing any power outputs and even *Motor* when it eventually got a Shadow for road test would only comment that 'the differences must be negligible' and didn't even hazard a guess as to just how much extra power and torque the revised engine produced. A portent of things to come was that American specification cars had a device which passed air into the exhaust system to ensure the fuel mixture was completely burnt.

The Camargue's debut in 1975 heralded a variation on the V8 theme. To distance the car further from other Rolls-Royces, David Plastow – who, as marketing director drove the project through – deemed it necessary that the Camargue should outperform others in the Rolls-Royce range. Therefore, from the 31st Camargue built a four-choke Solex 4A1 carburettor was fitted, except those destined for the USA and Japan where tighter emission regulations demanded twin SU HD8 carbs, 7.3:1 compression ratio and a catalyst. Lucas Opus breakerless ignition was adopted for the first time and the compression ratio lowered to 8.0:1 to permit the use of 98 octane fuel.

Two years on and the Shadow II debuted with yet more minor engine changes including smaller, 1.87 in diameter choke, SU HIF7 carbs replacing the older and bigger two-inch SU HD8s. A twin exhaust system, as used on the Corniche, helped to compensate for a potential loss in top end power caused by these US-specification carburetters. Others, including the Corniche, used the same four-choke Solex set up first seen on the Camargue.

Fuel injection finally made an appearance in a Crewe product in 1980 when Bosch K-Jetronic system was fitted to California-bound cars. The system became a standard fitting for all areas demanding Federal emission standards the following year, although it was going to be some time before EFI was fitted across the Rolls-Royce product range. Even unveiling the Shadow replacements, the Spirit and Spur, in 1980 was insufficient impetus to persuade Rolls-Royce technical team – headed by

John Hollings who took over from Grylls in 1968 – to switch over to electronic fuel injection. This conservatism, or shall we call it stubbornness?, was maintained in the face of increasing technical sophistication from rivals like Jaguar and Mercedes-Benz and, more importantly, ever more stringent exhaust emission and fuel consumption regulations which were being demanded by many of Rolls-Royce's overseas' markets, particularly the USA.

A management reorganisation in 1983 saw Mike Dunn take over as engineering director. Dunn was an outsider having forged his reputation as one of the leading figures behind Ford's then revolutionary Sierra. He was immediately aware that if something wasn't done then 'the best car in the world' would be Rolls-Royce's epitaph. Nevertheless, it wasn't until autumn 1986 that Rolls-Royce finally abandoned carburetters once and for all. At a casual glance it might seem that the only change to the 6.75-litre V8 was Bosch K-Jetronic mechanical fuel injection in place of carburetters, but delve a bit deeper and you suddenly become aware that this is practically a new engine. Starting at the bottom, the crankcase was stiffened by thickening the sump flange and adding a further rib while further development resulted in a stronger block with a new cross-tie on the engine/gearbox adaptor and further cross-bolting on the centre and two intermediate bearings. The wall between the fourth and fifth bearings was modified and improved cast iron liners fitted to reduce the chance of ovality and to decrease oil consumption. As well as changing the firing sequence to further improve refinement, the cylinder head was re-profiled to ease gas flow. Topping all this was a new two-tier manifold developed from known technology and designed to inject fuel at the valve to ensure precise fuel distribution. A thicker, 0.0039 mm against 0.0030 mm, head gasket was also fitted.

The mechanically timed high-energy ignition system remained unchanged, though the radiator and oil cooler were both enlarged for better engine cooling while the compression ratio remained at 8.0:1. Add all this up and the V8 now produced, unofficially, 238 bhp in the Spirit and Spur and marginally less in the Corniche. Since then, the venerable – don't forget it first appeared 34 years ago – V8 has remained unchanged. There was a flurry of excitement in the press in 1989 when Cosworth, which was subsequently bought by Rolls-Royce parent company, Vickers the following year, displayed a 32-valve cylinder head for the engine at the Autotech exhibition. But it remains doubtful if there were ever any plans to use this cylinder head as Rolls-Royce assiduously maintains its policy of only revealing major new developments at launch and not leaking them to the media.

Silver Cloud II and Phantom V

By the time Rolls-Royce unveiled its Cloud II in 1959, the basic concept was already eight years old although the original Cloud had been launched only four years earlier. Even then, the car was considered something of an anachronism as it still had a separate chassis and body at a time when unitary construction was being universally adopted. Such conservatism shouldn't have been a surprise as the car's principal designers – John Blatchley and Ivan Evernden working under Harry Grylls direction – were both steeped in Rolls-Royce traditions.

Before joining the Rolls-Royce power plant design office at Hucknall in 1939, Blatchley had been chief draughtsman and designer at Gurney Nutting, the Chelsea-based coachbuilders, while Evernden had worked alongside Sir Henry. With such close affiliations to coachbuilding traditions, combined with the fact that during the mid fifties there was still a strong coachbuilding presence in the UK, a separate chassis/body construction was the obvious way to go. What is, perhaps, less understandable is the Cloud's conservative design. It is an undeniably elegant car with its haughty, Phantomesque radiator and flowing wings, but even by the standards of the time it looks dated. It's worth noting that the wind-tunnel tuned R-Type Continental – surely one of the best-looking cars ever built? – was also penned by Evernden, which gives credence to the story that the then management moderated Evernden and Blatchley's original straight-through styling for the Cloud, although it was later seen on the S-Series Continentals.

Apart from gaining V8 power and some minor improvements, the Cloud II was essentially the same as its predecessor. Externally the two cars are virtually identical although keen eyed observers will note that V8s have black air intakes at the front; Rolls-Royce even retained the single exhaust pipe exiting by the left rear overrider. The box-section, cruciform chassis manufactured by John Thompson Motor Pressings of Wolverhampton came in three wheelbase lengths: 123 ins for the

The Silver Cloud's external appearance changed little over the years it was in production. Perhaps the Cloud's biggest update was getting a quartet of headlamps in the run-up to its replacement, the Silver Shadow. This is a 1965 convertible model

standard car, 127 ins for the long wheelbase and a mighty 145 ins for Phantom V and VI state limousines. Centralised lubrication was abandoned in favour of greasing points with individual reservoirs which needed replenishing every 10,000 miles or once a year. While the front track was 58.5 ins, half an inch up on the Cloud I, and the rear 60 ins. Suspension was independent at the front by double wishbones (now forged and machined rather than pressed steel), coil springs and hydraulic lever-arm dampers which also acted as inner fulcrums for the top wishbones and a stiffer anti-roll torsion bar. At the back, the live rear axle featured gaitered half-elliptic leaf springs, hydraulic dampers – which could be adjusted by the driver via a steering column-mounted switch – and a 'Z' bar to reduce spring wind-up under torque on the 123 and 127 ins chassis. Tyres were 8.20 x 15 ins mounted on six-inch steel disc wheels.

Even though some manufacturers had swopped to disc brakes, Rolls-Royce stubbornly kept with the old-fashioned drum set-up maintaining that it was just as efficient and quiet as the new system. But being Rolls-Royce this was no ordinary drum brake system … The unorthodox front brakes had twin, self-adjusting trailing shoes housed in heavily ribbed drums to prevent heat distortion while the linked – for even wear – rear shoe layout was a standard design. Power for the brakes was provided by a unique Rolls-Royce mechanical servo driven from the gearbox output shaft, a system first introduced by Sir Henry in 1925. Its one major disadvantage was a constant lag of about 18 ins; while this translates to about 1/50 sec at 50 mph and is hardly noticeable, 1/5 secs at 5 mph

could be potentially embarrassing driving in town or manoeuvring. This was despite gearing it up so that it rotated more quickly to reduce delays and altering the front-to-rear wheel braking ratio from 1.36 to 1.66:1. In all other respects it was a very efficient system, multiplying the driver's efforts sevenfold and extremley safe as it was connected into three independent linkages, two hydraulic and one mechanical. One master cylinder operated a single shoe in each front brake and supplied 76 per cent of the rear braking effort, with the balance provided by mechanical linkage which also served the handbrake, while the second master cylinder operated the front brakes' second shoes. If one component failed in any of the braking systems, the driver was still left with 65-85 per cent braking effort before resorting to the handbrake.

Pressure from customers, and the occasional disparaging press comment, prompted Rolls-Royce to make the Cloud II a more luxurious car than its predecessor. So we had power steering (3 2/3 turns lock-to-lock and a galleon-like 40 ft turning circle), standard for the first time. The cam-and-roller steering box was mounted further back and on the outside of the chassis frame due to the V8's extra girth and connected to the original steering column alignment by spiral input gears. Automatic transmission – optional on all Royces since 1952 – was now standard. Despite Rolls-Royce manufacturing the gearbox themselves it was GM's Hydramatic unit, which Cadillac first used in 1941, modified to take the mechanical brake servo. Unlike other autos of that period the Hydramatic was a four-speed unit, against the usual three, and had a fluid coupling instead of a torque convertor. The heating and ventilation system was redesigned so that for an extra £275 (plus taxes), owners could specify an airconditioning system which was located in and around and to the rear of the front off-side wheelarch.

Alas, fashions change and fewer people were prepared to commission and pay for bespoke bodies so that by the time the Cloud II was launched in October, 1959 the likes of Freestone & Webb, Hooper, Harold Radford, Abbott, Graber, Vanden Plas, Gurney Nutting and Franay were no more than memories. Of those that survived, H J Mulliner was taken over by Rolls-Royce in '59 and merged with Park Ward in 1961, which effectively left only the independent Italian carroserie, James Young and Mulliners to convert Silver Clouds. While the Italians seem to have ignored the car altogether, James Young was immersed in the Phantom V project, which practically counted them out, leaving just Mulliners.

In autumn, 1959 Mulliners unveiled an elegant convertible which was little more than a saloon with its roof lopped off and the rear doors missing. It was a car designed more for Florida or the Cote d'Azur than Brighton or Bournemouth as a power operated hood was an optional extra and it couldn't have been an easy or quick task to erect in a sudden

Right
Based on Silver Cloud III running gear this Mulliner Park-bodied convertible owes much in its concept to the original Cloud's design, which was turned down by Rolls-Royce' then management

Below right
Phantoms were also updated with twin headlamps at the same time as the Silver Cloud

cloud burst. Despite being pre-occupied with the Phantom V, James Young did build a number of two-door saloons based on the Cloud II. During its life, Rolls-Royce also produced a number of long-wheelbase chassis for James Young to clothe, while Mulliners produced a gracious four-door convertible which shows an uncanny resemblance to the Flying Spur. Park Ward were left to produce stretched versions of the standard steel saloon and such models are easily recognisable by the extra inches added to the rear doors. For those wanting complete privacy a central division could be specified as well as electric windows, which were still an option in those days – even for Rolls-Royce. Still, for those who wanted the ultimate in dignified personal transport Rolls-Royce could go even one better than a stretched Silver Cloud II – the Phantom V.

Between 1950 and '59, Rolls-Royce supplied Royalty and Heads of State with the straight-eight powered Phantom IV. A mighty car in more ways than one: its 5675 cc engine produced 162 bhp at 3750 rpm and 282 lb-ft torque at 1750 rpm, needing all of it to move the car's 5000 lbs kerb weight. There was only one snag, Rolls-Royce wouldn't entertain orders from members of the public To own a Phantom IV you had to be a Royal, like HM Queen who bought one while still HRH Princess Elizabeth, or a Head of State – Spain's Generalissimo Franco had three. Dukes and Duchesses counted as well, but any lesser title didn't stand a chance. You could, however, have purchased a long-wheelbase – 133 ins – Silver Wraith for coachwork conversion, but it still wasn't the ultimate car: that accolade belonged to the Phantom. But as the years passed it became increasingly obvious that the Phantom IV was living on borrowed time — especially as the new all-alloy V8 was due to replace the old straight-six.

So it was that visitors to the 1959 Earls Court Motor Show witnessed the launch of two cars which would have a continuing influence on British motoring: the Mini and the Phantom V. Despite bearing the Phantom name, the new state limousine – which would become available to everyone from pop stars to communist dictators – had no links with its predecessors bearing the same name; instead it was directly related to the Silver Cloud II. Effectively its chassis was a 22 ins stretched version of the Silver Cloud IIs, giving it a 145 ins wheelbase, though manufactured from heavier gauge steel. Other changes included a tube housing the propshaft, an extra inch on the front wishbones and a four-inch longer rear axle while the Cloud's rear Z-bar was omitted. Suspension was independent at the front by coil springs and wishbones and by asymmetric leaf springs at the back. The centralised lubrication system was dispensed with in favour of grease nipples while other inheritances from the Silver Cloud II included power steering and 11.25 x 3 ins drum brakes with the gearbox-driven mechanical servo. To cope with the demands of slow, processional speeds the final drive ratio was lowered to 3.89:1 compared to the Cloud II's 3.08:1. The standard Rolls-Royce/GM four-speed automatic transmission was used.

Although the number of independent coachbuilders was constantly shrinking there was sufficient demand from wealthy customers, who were intrigued by the combination of modern engineering and traditional coachbuilding techniques, for H J Mulliner, Park Ward, James Young and Hooper to produce proposals for Phantom V coachwork. In fact, Hooper never did build the car which its chief designer, Osmond Rivers, had conceived as they stopped coachbuilding in 1959 and Rivers' design was finally built by Henri Chaperon of Paris. Both Park Ward and James Young produced touring limousines as did H J Mulliner, though that was only a one-off, in addition to seven-passenger limousines. Because of its commitment to Bentley Continentals and convertible Silver Clouds, Mulliners produced relatively few Phantoms the most common being James Young – itself a subsidiary of the Jack Barclay group – and Park Ward which became the 'standard' Phantom V. At 19 ft 10 ins from bumper to bumper, 6 ft 7 ins wide and weighing in at 5600 lbs the Phantom was an extremely large car. Despite this massive bulk John Blatchley's styling has retained a period charm which once might have been considered dated, but can now be looked on as a classic. James Young's limousines betray more than a passing resemblance to contemporary Silver Clouds and even aped them as they went to a quad headlamp set-up with the Series III although, in the author's opinion, of all the early Phantoms the James Young sedanca de ville is the most elegant, especially with the roof section over the front, ie the chauffeur, removed. Above all, the Phantom is not what might be called a user/chooser car — it's designed for the chauffeured. Those seated in the back enjoy 63 ins of shoulder width and a limb-stretching 37.5 ins of leg room to the central partition. Even if the occasional seats are in use, there's plenty of leg room in the back. The chauffeur is less well catered for with firm upholstery, an upright seatback and not that much legroom if the driver tops six foot. Phantom V prices ranging from £8905 for the Park Ward limousine to £9394 for the James Young version would buy you a top-of-the-range Rover Metro nowadays, but in 1959 it was nearly 18 times the price of a new Mini ...

After only two years on the market, a re-styling exercise was undertaken to bring the Phantom in line with the Silver Cloud III which appeared in autumn, 1962. The SIII was beginning to show its age, not only externally but also under its curvaceous lines. The era of the mini-skirt was about to hit Rolls-Royce and they were still trying to sell a car which was designed when pop-socks and voluminous petticoats were all the rage. Project 'Burma' was at least three years away and sales were slipping; the Silver Cloud was looking a little bit tarnished. The most obvious visual change to the SIII was its Shadow-like front end with a quartet of 5 3/4 ins Lucas 150 watt headlights and flush-fitting indicator/side lamps replacing the SII's twin headlamps and sidelight pods. Those with a keen eye will also note that the radiator was lowered about 1.5 ins, thereby increasing the bonnet's forward rake. New overriders were also added, but only to UK specification models.

Under the bonnet the 6.25-litre engine received a seven per cent power hike as already detailed, but the most significant change was to interior dimensions. After seven years front bench seats had been done away with and replaced with more comfortable and more supportive individual chairs while the rear seat had more upright squabs which afforded an additional two inches of legroom and slimmer corner bolsters for extra width. Otherwise the car remained virtually the same – apart from increased power assistance – even down to the drum brakes and mechanical servo which got panned in a *Motor* road test for increased pedal pressure. To be fair the magazine re-tested the car after Rolls-Royce had re-set the brakes, but it underlined how outmoded this technology had become.

Coachwork variations on the Cloud III not only included long-wheelbase versions, but also drophead coupés from H J Mulliner and – following the company's integration with Park Ward, when the two had been taken over by Rolls-Royce – a very elegant two- and four-door Flying Spur with practically straight-through wing styling. The Cloud's mechanical updates were incorporated in Phantom Vs from 1962 onwards together with detailed styling changes which included chromium-plated window frames and door tops and rounded corners to the front quarterlights as well as a re-profiled tail with a razor-edged appearance. But the most obvious update was the adoption of the Cloud's quartet of headlights and the deletion of the front wings' topmost swage line which caused manufacturing problems. The previous year Park Ward delivered its first landaulette – a sort of demi-convertible with the passenger's section of the roof folding back – to the Governor of Hong Kong. A second landaulette – still with single headlights – was built for 'Mrs Stirling' (better known as the Queen Mother), the following year complete with intercom between passengers and chauffeur. And if you're still wondering how and why the Phantom V has influenced every motorist in the UK, it's 238 inch overall length dictated the size of British parking meter bays.

Even with its hood in place the car's 'straight-through' styling and quartet of slanted headlamps produces a very elegant design

Silver Shadow

It is fitting that Harry Grylls, who became chief engineer at Rolls-Royce in 1951 and was one of the last links with Sir Henry Royce, should have been responsible for the marque's first truly modern post-war design. Gryll's association with the company started when his father purchased an early Rolls-Royce. After Rugby and Trinity College, Cambridge, Grylls junior joined Rolls-Royce in 1930, aged 21, and was fortunate enough to work alongside Sir Henry at West Wittering. Royce's obsession with perfection must have rubbed off on the young Grylls as he instigated the 'Burma' and 'Tibet' programmes, one of which would eventually replace the Silver Cloud in 1965, as early as 1956-57. Nowadays any car producer would scoff at the idea of taking a decade to design and develop a car – excluding the powertrain – but in the mid fifties, Grylls obviously concurred with Shakespeare's dictum that 'Wisely and slowly: they stumble that run fast'.

Once again it was Evernden and Blatchley who got the ball rolling with a number of feasibility studies – including a front-wheel drive proposal which would have been an intriguing prospect, to say the least – which all had a common theme: monocoque construction. Following a visit to Detroit, Evernden was convinced that monocoque bodies with subframe mountings for the suspension was the only engineering/design route Rolls-Royce could pursue. The first of three 'Tibet' prototypes took to the roads in August 1958. It wasn't a small a car, measuring 210 ins in length and 72 ins wide, which probably sealed its fate as in the previous spring a more compact saloon had emerged; Project 'Burma' measured 195 ins from bumper to bumper, 70 ins between the wheelarches, had a 119.5 ins wheelbase and, most importantly, at 3643 lbs was 781 lbs lighter than 'Tibet'. 'Burma' was given the go-ahead and by 1960 the first prototypes were undergoing tests, the wheelbase increased by an inch to accommodate the new V8 engine which had appeared in the Silver Cloud II the previous year.

With the emergence of the Silver Shadow, Rolls-Royce signalled the end of the traditional separate chassis/coachbuilt bodies that had been its trademark since the company was formed. When Project 'Burma' was

In 1965, the original Rolls-Royce Silver Shadow prototype shows a distinct change of style from its predecessor. Above all this model represented Rolls-Royce graduation into modern car design with its monocoque construction

Above

White wall tyres date this picture which was used by Rolls-Royce as one of its press shots when the Silver Shadow was launched

Left

An early interior shot of a left-hand drive Silver Shadow. Times might have changed, but Rolls-Royce owners clearly still demanded a traditional blend of wood and leather

finally unveiled in autumn 1965 it was quite unlike any previous Rolls-Royce and one that answered all the criticisms levelled at the Silver Cloud III ... well almost all of them. Unfortunately, customers would have to wait until the following spring before deliveries were made and 18 months before the likes of *Autocar* and *Motor* got one to test.

The biggest breakthrough in the Shadow's design was its monocoque construction produced by the Pressed Steel Company, the only non-steel components being the aluminium closing panels.

Despite the powertrain being essentially the same as the Cloud's, Rolls-Royce took the opportunity to modify both. The engine changes have been detailed elsewhere while the GM four-speed auto was updated for the domestic market by making the main castings from aluminium instead of cast iron and adding a freewheel to first and second to improve shifts. While the mechanical gearchange linkage was replaced by an electrically actuated system. Left-hand drive models got the GM400 (TurboHydramatic), three-speed auto with torque convertor which

eventually became standard across the range and, unlike, its predecessor was built by GM to Rolls-Royce's precise requirements. The only addition Crewe made to the gearbox was installing an actuator for the electronic gearchange. It wasn't only the gearchange which was electrically powered: front seats, rear window demister, door windows, aerial and the petrol filler flap were electrically-operated. And, as an illustration of Crewe's attention to detail, the four sealed beam headlamps had a safety relay so that if all the mainbeam filaments went out, dipped beam switched in automatically, and vice versa.

Old-fashioned as separate chassis/body construction might be, it does ensure that passengers are isolated from mechanical and road-induced noise, vibration and harshness. But with monocoque construction, where the suspension and powertrain are mounted directly to the passenger cell, there is a danger that the body will act as an amplifier. In an effort to minimise this problem, Grylls and his team installed Vibrashock mountings between the subframes and the body. But while effective in reducing NVH they increased compliance in the suspension which, combined with some horizontal movement from the front subframe, quickly led to complaints of mushy steering and handling.

While the powertrain might have been virtual carryovers from the Cloud, the Shadow's suspension and braking systems were as

Above
Despite the growing sophistication of its rivals, Rolls-Royce retained, in many ways, a stubborn conservatism: while the new Shadow might have boasted monocoque construction and, at last, disc brakes it ran on cross-ply tyres

Above right
'Coke-bottle' styling might be considered passé nowadays, but these early Corniches have a timeless elegance which few modern cars possess

Right
Although classed as a four-seater, those in the back have insufficient leg room for long journeys. Anyway, with a car as elegant as this why would you want more company than your own partner?

sophisticated as Rolls-Royce could design. The suspension – double wishbones and anti-roll bar at the front and semi-trailing arms at the back with coil spring over dampers at each corner – was augmented by a hydraulic ram, running at 1150 psi, located between the top of the damper and the bodyshell. Interconnected from side-to-side there was no front-to-back link, although the system was designed to be self-levelling with three inches of vertical travel at the rear and an inch at the front (later discontinued). The brakes, too, represented a departure from tradition. Not only were discs used for the first time, but Sir Henry's gearbox-driven servo was absent for the first time in more than 40 years. Eleven inch diameter Girling discs were used all round with twin calipers at the front and single ones for the rear discs. In an effort to reduce brake squeal each disc had a soft iron wire wrapped loosely round its outer edge, secured by a steel band, the theory being that the vibration in the disc would cause slip between these components thus creating friction damping. High pressure hydraulic fluid provided the braking effort, but in typical Rolls-Royce fashion an ordinary master cylinder was linked to the brake pedal, not only to give the driver some feel, but also to act as a third line of defence should the brakes fail. Such a calamity was highly unlikely as one system provided 47 per cent of braking effort (split 31/16 front-to-rear), the second 31 per cent to the front brakes and the remaining 23 per cent from the master cylinder to the rear wheels. To further complicate matters each of the front calipers was fed by its own high pressure system and one pair of the rear caliper's four pots was fed by the second high pressure system and the second pair by the conventional master cylinder.

Despite all of this technology, the new Rolls-Royce didn't really further the cause of ride and handling. Sitting on cross-ply tyres and with all the compliance built into the suspension the Shadow was more at home on America's long and straight turnpikes than sweeping British 'A' roads. The introduction of monocoque construction virtually spelt the end for traditional coachbuilders as Rolls-Royce were reluctant to supply unfinished bodyshells to outside concerns. But in one last flourish James Young produced 35 two-door Shadows between 1965 and '67 which were little more than four-door cars with the rear doors removed, new panels inserted and larger front doors used. Body lines were identical to the Crewe-built cars and, in reality, they are an inadequate epitaph for a company with such a long and distinguished past.

Meanwhile, Rolls-Royce's own coachbuilders were going from strength to strength. In autumn, 1965, H J Mulliner, Park Ward offered a second version of the State Laundaulette in which the rear roof portion retracted further uncovering more of the occupants. Not only that, but the rear seat could be electrically raised by 3.5 ins so the public could

Above
The stark modernity of Munich's Olympic village contrasts strongly with the classic lines of the Rolls-Royce radiator

Right
The sudden explosion of wealth in the Middle East following the second oil crises assured Rolls-Royce of a new, untapped market which the company fully exploited

get a better view of the dignitaries in the car. Crewe's reluctance to supply outsiders with unfinished Shadow floorpans or bodyshells might have something to do with the 1966 announcement of its own two-door saloon. The elegant Bill Allen-penned car was pure Silver Shadow mechanicals and floor pan, but the coachwork was produced at Mulliner Park Ward's Hythe Road, Willesden factory. But the build sequence was one of the most illogical in the motor industry – though it managed to survive for 25 years: the floorpans and body components were delivered to Hythe Road where they were jig-assembled. The completed shells were transported to Crewe where they received rustproofing, undercoats, powertrain, hydraulics, electrics etc, after which the rolling chassis were sent back to Hythe Road where the hood was finished, interior trimmed out and the final paint added. In total it took some 20 weeks to build a two-door saloon and not much longer for a convertible (which was introduced in 1967).

It is easy to see why the two-door has remained virtually unchanged over the past 25 years; the slight, but elegant, kick over the rear wheels accentuated by the swage line down the flanks. That and the re-profiled bootline and rear lights give the car a more purposeful, almost sporting stance. Inside it's virtually a two-seater, though a pair of adults can be squeezed into the back seats for short journeys. Hythe Road must have been buzzing in those days as in 1968 the Phantom VI appeared. Although a number of proposals were put forward for a more radical update of the P5 – including one that incorporated discs brakes, a de-

toxed engine, central locking, powered doors etc, which would have allowed US sales – the eventual revamp was only subtly different. The only distinguishing alteration to the exterior was an intake grille at the base of the windscreen. But under the noble bodywork there were a number of mechanical updates: the 6230 cc V8 from the Silver Shadow was now used and the PVI became the first car in the world to be fitted with twin independent airconditioning units; a Silver Shadow system for the chauffeur's compartment, which also benefitted from a revised fascia, and a separate system for the rear passengers. The PVI also became the first British car to cost more than £10,000, excluding taxes. When purchase tax was added the total bill for a 'standard' Phantom VI was £12,843 and 15 shillings.

While all this was going on, Crewe was also undertaking a series of minor improvements to the Shadow; a stiffer front anti-roll bar was fitted and, for the first time, a rear anti-roll bar installed in an effort to sharpen up the car's handling while the front suspension's ride-levelling system was deleted. More significant was adopting the GM400 torque convertor auto across the range – it had always been fitted to left-hand drive Shadows – in place of the old Hydramatic. This new policy also meant that the gearboxes, complete with the electric actuator, were now built by GM and shipped to Crewe.

Above
This 1975 anniversary edition of the Silver Shadow featured Georgian silver coachwork offset by red fine lines and was specially built for overseas's customers

Above right
Grey Connolly interior with red piping and Wilton carpeting, offset by the veneer fascia and top rails epitomise Rolls-Royce approach to interior styling

Right
Rear passenger comfort has always been of paramount importance to Rolls-Royce. Note the wide-opening doors for easy access and the passengers' footrests

For those not quite in the Phantom's price-bracket there was always the long-wheelbase Shadow introduced in 1969. With an extra four inches in the wheelbase, between the 'B' and 'C' posts, the Wraith was available with and without an electrically-powered division. Those cars fitted with a division came with twin airconditioning units. Only keen R-R spotters can tell a Wraith at a glance; its most distinguishing feature over a Shadow was the 'Everflex' roof covering, longer rear doors and linked R badges on the 'C' posts. The rear window was also reduced in size. So discreet was the Wraith that a prototype was delivered to Princess Margaret in 1967 for her own personal use.

All R-R models – Shadow, Wraith and the two-doors – benefited from having the US-specification fascia with its extra padding and re-organised minor controls and instruments standardised across all markets. For a manufacturer who supposedly doesn't do very much between new model announcements, Rolls-Royce was very active during this period. For example, in 1970, as has been detailed elsewhere, the V8's capacity was increased to 6.75 litres and introduced in MY'71 and the two-door Shadows were relaunched as the Corniche, but with significant mechanical changes.

But before the March 1972 launch got underway disaster struck. Rolls-Royce Aeroengines, the car producers parent company, went into

Above
This splendid blue state landaulette was the seventh built by Rolls-Royce and delivered in 1976

Above right
By 1977, when this picture was taken, the Corniche had undergone subtle changes: impact-absorbing bumpers had replaced the more elegant chrome ones and a discreet spoiler had been added to the front

Right
A formal Phantom VI at the 1979 NEC Motor Show

receivership, crippled by the spiralling costs of developing its 'big fan' RB.211 jet engine for the Lockheed TriStar.

Visually the Corniche differed little from its predecessor: a deeper radiator shell, new wheel trims and a modest 'Corniche' badge on the car's rump. Under the bonnet was the 6.75-litre V8, although those for the US made do with the Shadow's de-toxed engine, while the driver had a new wood-rimmed steering wheel, an updated fascia incorporating a rev counter and a revised centre console.

A year after the RB.211 debacle, by which time Rolls-Royce Motorcars Ltd was an independent company with David Plastow as its managing director, the Shadow's suspension underwent minor modifications in another attempt to quell the growing criticisms of the car's inadequate handling. The fundamental problem lay in the compliant Vibrashock mountings, so these were discarded in favour of stiffer rubber bushes. A cranked-arm top link, which was triangulated to the subframe by a compression strut, replaced the wide-based top wishbones at the front while the Panhard Rod located between the monocoque and the subframe was also discarded. Radial-ply tyres were fitted for the first time and the front wheel track increased to 59.4 ins.

Not only was the Shadow subjected to a constant programme of updates, but so was the Phantom. In 1972, the rear doors were re-

Above
The Phantom VI could be classed as the world's last, truly coachbuilt car. Although some cars are still handmade, the PVI was the last direct link to the old coach building tradition of separate bodies and chassis

Above right
The 16th and possibly the grandest state landaulette built. Ordered by Jack Barclay Ltd for a Far Eastern customer it had additional bright metalwork and recessed rear lights. Those doors crests are solid 24 carat gold

Right
Two magnificent examples of British engineering: the Forth Bridge and a Corniche II convertible

Above

Rarer, though no less elegant, the Corniche saloon is one of those few designs where adding a permanent roof to a convertible hasn't spoiled the overall aesthetics

Right

The Corniche has always been a firm favourite with America, especially the sunshine states of California and Florida where most Corniche users never put the hood down preferring, instead, the full benefits of airconditioning

designed so they hinged from the front rather than the back and burst-proof locks capable of withstanding 30G fitted, while a collapsible steering column and a more effective handbrake together with other safety items brought the PVI into line with European safety regulations. Disc brakes, already standard on the Corniche, appeared on Shadows in '73 as well as a myriad of minor cosmetic improvements including a better central-locking system, a new cruise control and a courtesy light delay. Shock-absorbing bumpers to suit American demands appeared and the bottom edge of the grille raised to accommodate the new front bumper; the rectangular grilles beneath the headlights were also deleted. The suspension received another tweak with lower profile tyres – 235/70-15 ins – and the rear track increased by 2.875 ins thanks to new, longer semi-trailing arms which also had the effect of extending the wheelbase to 120 ins. If all this activity wasn't enough, Crewe's engineers were also developing a new car under the code-name 'Delta'.

Camargue

Traditional, independent coachbuilding might have virtually disappeared in the UK, but Rolls-Royce was determined the custom should continue. By the late 1960s the management decided to replace the coachbuilt two-door Corniche saloon with something more distinctive.

In a break from tradition, Rolls-Royce approached the Italian designer, Sergio Pininfarina to pen the new car. But he didn't start with a completely clean sheet of paper; the new coupé had to be a four-seater offering the same interior accommodation as the Shadow. Not only that, but it would be based on virtually unaltered Shadow floorpan and running gear which dictated that Pininfarina couldn't alter any of the hard points such as scuttle height at the base of the windscreen or the engine height.

The first drawings were seen by the R-R management team in October 1969, and by the end of the following year Pininfarina had full-size mockups of the interior and exterior ready for viewing by the directors. While the exterior needed some tweaking, especially the Italians' treatment of the R-R grille, the interior met with almost universal approval and acceptance. Pininfarina had created a luxurious, modern atmosphere with a quartet of individually sculptured seats and a distinctive new aircraft-like fascia, created by the simple expediency of putting square blackplates round the circular instruments. The interior was trimmed in 450 sq ft of a new Connolly hide, Nuella, supplied exclusively to Rolls-Royce for the Camargue.

Although Pininfarina had no Rolls-Royce design experience, he had produced a two-door coupé based on a Bentley T-series at the 1968 Paris Salon which was eventually bought by James (now Lord), Hanson. The similarity between that and the elegant Fiat 130 Coupé of the same period – also styled by Pininfarina – are obvious.

In many ways the Camargue contained a number of technological innovations Crewe had been working on for a number of years. Amongst the 'firsts' were the curved stainless steel – in place of the more usual chromium-plated brass – window frames and the glued-in windscreen. The Camargue was, incidentally, the first Rolls-Royce to use curved glass in the side windows. But the most noticeable innovation was the world's

Ancient and modern: the Pininfarina-designed Camargue two-door with a 1905 10 hp Rolls-Royce in the background. The latter is the oldest car owned by the factory

first split-level automatic airconditioning system which enabled the driver to set a separate, cooler temperature for his head and a warmer setting for the footwells and rear passengers which would be automatically maintained irrespective of the outside temperature. This enormously powerful system with its nine kW heat output and the cooling capacity of 30 domestic refrigerators cost the equivalent of a new Mini when the car was eventually launched in 1975.

I say 'eventually' because its debut was delayed by three factors: (a), the parent company's financial collapse (b), a prolonged strike in 1973 at the London works and (c), the need to facilitise a new production facility at the ex-Triplex site which was close to Hythe Road.

Like the Corniche the Camargue followed the same London-Crewe-London build process, but in this instance it took nearly six months as the numerous body pressings took a considerable amount of time to bring up to Rolls-Royce exacting standards. And what should have been simple operations, like fitting the rear seat squab, would take at least a working day. The Camargue's powertrain was derived from the Corniche two-door it supplemented — 6.75-litre engine and three-speed auto —

Pininfarina's styling borrowed heavily from the Fiat 130 Coupé which he penned at the same time and a one-off coupé based on a Bentley T-series shown at the Paris Salon in 1968

The USA always had a love affair with the Camargue. Perhaps because it was the most expensive car on sale in the USA – don't forget that Phantoms weren't sold in the 'States

while its underpinnings came from the revised Shadow with its 120 ins wheelbase, 60 ins front track and 59.6 ins rear track. But Plastow was dissatisfied with the car's performance as the Camargue was intended to be the quickest Rolls-Royce available, yet its 1/4-mile time of 17.7 secs was half a second slower than the Corniche two-door. To counteract that and increase the car's 118 mph top speed, the twin SU HD8 carbs fitted to the first 30 cars were replaced by a four barrel Solex 4A1 carburetter with fixed chokes.

When you realise that its UK launch price of £29,250 made the Camargue twice as expensive as the Shadow – and at US $90,000 America's most costly car – it is hardly surprising to learn that only one per week was produced.

Even during the Camargue's gestation, Crewe's engineering department was beavering away at improving both the Corniche and Shadow: the Corniche – which had received shock-absorbing bumpers for the US market in 1974 as well as other minor cosmetic changes – now got the Camargue's split-level airconditioning and the same four-barrel Solex carburetter set up. The braking system on both the

Left
Pininfarina's styling was always going to be a compromise as the Camargue is based entirely on Shadow running gear

Right
Perhaps the unhappiest aspects of the car is its bluff frontal appearance and vast, featureless bonnet

Corniche and Shadow dispensed with the conventional back-up hydraulic circuit and made do with just the two high-pressure systems.

But 1977 was to be the Shadow's big year. Apart from the very minor cosmetic changes which had been made to the Shadow and Wraith since its launch 12 years earlier it was, essentially, the same car. It had proved a spectacular sales success – in Rolls-Royce terms – with more than 3000 cars sold in 1975, so there was a natural reluctance to replace it. Nevertheless, improvements were needed and with the Shadow's replacement not due for a number of years the facelift would have to be quite considerable if the model range was to maintain its sales popularity in the face of increasing competition from the likes of Mercedes-Benz and Jaguar.

Above
For a coupé the Camargue is a very big car, in fact it will seat four adults in more than reasonable comfort

Left
The dramatic aircraft-style instrumentation was achieved by the simple expediency of putting new surrounds on standard Rolls-Royce instrumentation

Owners in the Middle East must have been especially appreciative of the Camargue's automatic bi-level airconditioning system. Early versions of the Camargue proved disappointingly slow when compared to the two-door Corniche. Installing a new carburetter fixed that problem. Camargue production was painfully slow, even by Rolls-Royce standards, taking up to six months for each car to be completed. Eventually Camargue production was consolidated at Crewe in a special facility away from the main production area. Although a Bentley Turbo version of the Camargue was developed it never reached production, although the engine did in the original Bentley Mulsanne Turbo

Above
Unique red and white Nuella leather trim was used in each of the dozen
commemorative cars described below

Right
A double celebration: to commemorate the 80th anniversary of Charles Rolls' first
demonstration of a Rolls-Royce in the USA a limited edition of 12 Camargues were
built in 1986. These cars also marked the end of Camargue build of which 390, or 74
per cent of production, had gone to the States

Silver Shadow & Wraith Series II

Visually there is little to distinguish the Silver Shadow and Wraith II from its predecessors: an air dam beneath the front bumper – which the Camargue got as well – and more prominent wraparound safety bumpers (located on deformable mild steel brackets for the UK market), twin exhaust pipes and a boot-mounted badge which proclaimed you were following the latest Rolls-Royce saloon. The keenest of observer would have noted that the grille was 0.47 ins deeper – the same as US specification cars.

But beneath the surface Rolls-Royce made no fewer than 1659 modifications to the car – many in an effort to quell the growing criticism of the car's roly-poly handling. Starting at the front, and working our way rearwards, we find rack-and-pinion steering in place of recirculating ball. The Burman system had been under development at Crewe for three years and, unusually, features central take offs with long links to the steering arms so that the previous model's steering geometry could be retained. The front subframe was also modified to give more swing axle effect by raising the upper 'wishbones' mounting point. This resulted in keeping the wheel more upright relative to the road under cornering and lowering the roll angle. To balance the handling still further the diameter of the rear anti-roll bar was reduced. The engine changes have been described in detail elsewhere, but were primarily designed to cope with growing emission legislation while maintaining the V8's power output.

Inside passengers would have noticed quite a change between the Shadow I and II. The adoption of the Camargue-style airconditioning system meant a redesign for the fascia with a new warning light display to the right and new instrumentation. The AE Econocruise speed control was now located in the gear selector mechanism and, because the cruise control was now electronic it meant that the Vdo/Jaeger speedo could also be electrified, making this Rolls-Royce the first British car to be fitted with a non-mechanical speedometer which, incidentally, read to

From head-on it is relatively easy to distinguish the 'mark II' Shadow with its spoiler, spot lights and – on this later model – toothbrush-style headlamp cleaners

999,999 miles. The fascia itself was a thin veneer of wood mounted on a light alloy panel to comply with safety regulations.

The centre console was redesigned to house the radio and tape deck, and driver's would have found themselves confronted by a smaller, 15.25 ins, steering wheel thanks to the new steering rack. The long-wheelbase model, now christened the Wraith II, was also updated the only change being fixed front seats if the car was ordered with the electric division between front and rear passengers.

Although most of Crewe's attentions and efforts had been concentrated on getting the Shadow II into production the other models weren't forgotten, especially the Camargue. Ever since its launch, Rolls-Royce had been unhappy with the problems it had experienced in building the Camargue to their own precise standards. So, in 1978 body build was transferred to Motor Panels in Coventry who assembled the monocoques which were then delivered to Crewe for rustproofing and painting on the same production line as the saloons. Final assembly, however, took place in a unique Camargue facility at Crewe following the decision to slim down the London operation.

Meanwhile the Corniche convertible benefitted from all the mechanical changes which had been made to the Shadow as well as getting the new style fascia. Visually the car remained virtually the same except for the addition of a front spoiler on all models bar those destined for the States.

Updating the Phantom VI continued so that by now it was powered

Above

Long-wheelbase versions of the Shadow ll could be distinguished by the standard vinyl roof covering, the badging on the 'C' posts and the smaller rear window

Right

This rear three-quarter view of a Silver Wraith ll shows the extended wheelbase and increased rear legroom

by the 6.75-litre engine, had the GM400 gearbox and power brakes. The latter, incidentally, were still 11.25 ins x 3 ins drums as fitting the Shadow's disc system would have meant redesigning the axles and bearings. However, the Shadow's hydraulics were modified to operate the Phantom's twin master cylinders via power rams. Nineteen Seventy-Eight saw the most famous Phantom of all delivered. To celebrate HM The Queen's Silver Jubilee the Society of Motor Manufacturers & Traders presented her with a unique high-roofed PVI, with a special Perspex dome and light-alloy cover, on a four-headlamp body. Other special fittings included an extra wide armrest for a cassette recorder, radio and airconditioning controls. The usual cocktail cabinet was replaced with additional cassette storage and an Asprey clock. A unique airconditioning system was also installed with additional air outlets and a booster which allows rear compartment heating even when the front heating controls are switched off. As with other Royal Phantoms used overseas, this car's bumpers may be removed to allow easy storage in the Royal Yacht

Above

By the late 1970s – this is a MY'77 Wraith II – two-tone paintwork was much in vogue. This side elevation clearly shows the extended rear doors

Left

Two-tone paintwork suits the Corniche, highlighting the swage line running down its flanks

Britannia's garage. The statistically-minded might like to note that despite running on standard section 8.90-15 ins cross ply tyres, this PVI tips the scales at 6790 lbs and has a quoted maximum payload of 1300 lbs; which means it can weigh over 8000 lbs fully laden.

In 1979 Rolls-Royce made the most significant change to any of its models following the Shadow II's appearance, yet it was only available on the Corniche and they didn't tell anyone about it. Crewe's products were coming under increasing scrutiny, especially from the media, who often complained that despite being considerably more expensive, Shadows, Corniches and Camargues were inferior to Mercedes-Benz and, especially, Jaguar when it came to ride, handling and tyre/road noise suppression. Stung into action, Crewe's ride and handling experts set to work revising the rear suspension by linking together the subframes for the semi-trailing arm pivots and the final drive assembly. Additionally, the semi-trailing arm pivot angle went from 16 degrees to 21 degrees 38 minutes, wheel tracks were marginally increased, springs were shortened

and softened while the gas struts were relocated behind the line of the drive shafts. Mineral oil replaced brake fluid in the hydraulic systems and, in 1980 and for the Californian market only, fuel injection made its first appearance in a Rolls-Royce.

The new decade also spelt the end of an era for Rolls-Royce: the Corniche two-door saloon ceased production, though the last model wasn't completed until spring of the following year, and after 15 glorious years Shadow production stopped to make way for a new, more modern Rolls-Royce saloon.

Whatever its setting the Corniche looks a truly regal car; and redesigned rear suspension ensured that in 1979 the handling lived up to the looks. Always a personal aesthetic judgement - and not necessarily true of many cars described as 'timeless', even cars from Crewe - the Corniche does not date

Above

A change in name is all that really distinguishes this car – a Corniche II two-door – from a Shadow two-door

Above right

Corniche two-doors found favour with the European market. This is one of the later models with the front spoiler and toothbrush-style headlamp wash/wipe system

Right

The Shadow was the company's first real export success, finding plenty of buyers in Europe as well as further overseas

Above

Typically, Wraith's tended to be more chauffeur driven than 'user/chooser' Shadows

Left

Originally Shadows had good old-fashioned chrome bumpers and overriders, but these had to be dispensed with when legislation demanded more pedestrian-friendly impact-absorbing bumpers with rubber inserts

Silver Spirit, Spur & other derivatives

The 1970s had been a traumatic decade for the motor industry. Since the end of World War 2 car sales had grown steadily. The consumer society was booming with new wealth; and a willingness to spend on luxury goods had ensured that Rolls-Royce – together with other top league producers such as Aston Martin, Jaguar, Mercedes-Benz etc – were enjoying unparalleled levels of success. What is more, it didn't cost that much to run these cars. Petrol was readily available and cheap, it didn't matter that fuel consumption for these luxury cars was in the teens. Furthermore exhaust emissions were just becoming an issue and even then only in California – which had already got itself something of a reputation as a fringe society with eccentric ideas. But all this calm was shattered with not one, but two oil crises, which sent the price of oil-based products rocketing. Fuel consumption became an issue and suddenly cars such as Rolls-Royces were seen as profligate, squandering the earth's vital and limited resources. In fact, the oil crises claimed many smaller independent manufacturers – such as Jensen and Iso – who used gas-guzzling American V8s in their luxury, high-performance GTs.

The knock-on effect of these crises was worsening economies. Suddenly people became conscious of wealth and openly displaying it – unlike the late 1920s and early '30s when the rich carried on as though there was no depression – and the sale of luxury items declined. With such social turmoil, it might not have been unreasonable to think that Rolls-Royce should have considered 'downsizing' its next generation of products. And, indeed, a number of such programmes were investigated by Crewe only for the same answers to keep coming up: the rich were only delaying the purchase of their next Royce. Part of a Rolls-Royce's appeal was its size and grandeur – smaller cars didn't have the same cachet or prestige. So, taking these elements into account – plus the fact that Crewe had been working on the Shadow's replacement since 1974 and couldn't afford to scrap the programme and start from scratch –

A new decade dawns and with it a new generation of Rolls-Royce saloons. The Silver Spirit, essentially, was a re-skinned Shadow and surprised many commentators by not being any smaller or lighter than the car it superseded

makes it inevitable that when the Silver Spirit appeared in October 1980 it was no smaller or lighter than the car it replaced. In fact to many observers the Fritz Feller styled car – code-named SZ – looked bigger than its predecessor, and they weren't wrong: the Spirit was 2.9 ins longer and 2.3 ins wider than the Shadow. On the more positive side its 120.5 ins wheelbase was an inch greater and its roofline 1.25 ins lower, while there had been a 30 per cent increase in glass area.

The long-wheelbase model, now called the Silver Spur, sported a 124.5 ins wheelbase which was an inch up on the Wraith it replaced. Underneath the bodyshell it was virtually Silver Shadow II componentry: the floorpan and drivetrain were unaltered as was the front suspension while the rear suspension with its softer springs and redesigned subframes was identical to that which first appeared on the Corniche in 1979. This policy of evolution rather than revolution continued in the cabin where the fascia was a mild reworking of the Shadow II's, the only real difference being that the analogue clock and outside temperature gauge were replaced by a digital readout for air temperature, current time and a stopwatch.

Other minor improvements included more heavily bolstered and shaped seating and, thanks to the broader 'C' posts, larger vanity mirrors. Increasing safety legislation had forced Rolls-Royce to dispense with the back seat's veneered picnic tables – although these reappeared later with thick padding on the outer surface – and to adopt a novel solution to prevent the 'Flying Lady' from injuring any pedestrian unfortunate enough to be involved in an accident with a Rolls-Royce: on impact the spring-loaded Spirit of Ecstasy would retract into the radiator shell where the statuette would stay until pulled back into position. This neat solution also had the added benefit of making the 'Flying Lady' almost impossible to steal.

To many observers the Spirit looked too anonymous to be a real Rolls-Royce. True, it is an imposing car on the road, but its slab-sided lines lack flair which the car's slight waisting and kick-up over the rear arches fail to disguise. That and the shape of the large, rectangular headlights repeated in the full-width lamp assembly across the car's rear led many commentators to remark that the Spirit was more Volvo than Rolls-Royce. Yet, despite its outwardly modern appearance the Spirit kept some curiously old-fashioned links with the past: the window frames, for instance, were constructed from a multitude of components which, if not properly adjusted, would bow outwards under high-speed

Fritz Feller was responsible for designing the Silver Spirit which is longer, wider and lower than the Shadow and also has an increased glass area

Above

Rear seats in the Spirit were much more heavily bolstered than those in the Shadow. Fold down picnic tables are absent in this example, but footrests and lambswool carpeting aren't

Right

A Silver Spur in one of its natural environments; Beverly Hills (Picture: Colin Burnham)

pressure. The fascia's ergonomics – never a Rolls-Royce strong point – hadn't improved at all. Meanwhile the company itself was going through traumatic changes. While it had maintained its independence through the 1970s, the next decade didn't look so promising – a suitable partner had to be found. Consequently, in a convoluted deal Rolls-Royce chief David Plastow became chief executive of Vickers – the armaments and engineering conglomerate – and the two companies merged in the hope that they would provide mutual support for the years ahead.

The early 1980s were not a generous time for Rolls-Royce. Declining sales, redundancies and strikes severely restricted investment in new product and, it must be said, the partnership with Vickers didn't bring the sound bedrock that had been hoped for. Consequently few changes were made to the cars: in 1981 the Camargue received fuel-injection and in 1985 Robert Jankel Design were commissioned by Rolls-Royce to produce four- and six-door Spurs with a 36-inch stretch specifically for

Above

Additional rear legroom is immediately obvious in this picture of an early Spur's back seat. As with the Spirit, picnic tables are absent and the doors lack capping rails

Left

The Middle East proved a strong market for Rolls-Royce during the oil-boom eighties. Note that this early Spirit still has the old-style toothbrush headlamp wipers rather than jet washers

the American and other overseas markets. But most of the effort – financial and manpower – was going into re-establishing the Bentley marque which had virtually fallen into disuse over the past decade or so. The changes that were made for the MY'85 Silver Spirits were purely cosmetic: powered washers replacing the old toothbrush-style headlamp wash/wipe system, electrically-heated door mirrors, the radio aerial repositioned to the rear nearside wing and, inside, a centre console housing controls for the door mirrors and seat adjustment while deeper walnut waistrails and repositioned armrests were also included.

Meanwhile the coachbuilding fraternity was coming back to life. Encouraged, perhaps, by RJD's example the long-established coachbuilding firm of Hoopers revealed a two-door Spirit in 1985 with 8.5 ins longer front doors and a smaller rear window. The interior got the full bespoke treatment, too, with a quartet of individual seats, a through centre console running from front to rear and wood colour-

keyed to match the paintwork. These conversions tended to be performed on cars already registered by their owners – otherwise it would infringe Type Approval regulations – who originated from the Middle and Far East. And, while the factory might not have approved of such conversions there was nothing it could do to prevent them taking place.

Nineteen Eighty-Five was significant for Rolls-Royce as its 100,000th car was built – 81 years after the company had been founded. To celebrate the occasion 25 replicas of that 100,000th car – a royal blue Silver Spur – were commissioned. The Silver Spur Centenary models were trimmed in champagne-coloured hide and dark blue carpets with monogrammed waist rails on the door cappings, inlaid picnic tables, engraved door sill plates and a commemorative plaque in the glove box. Each owner also received a radiator-shaped presentation case containing a silver keyring, silver ballpoint pen and a notepad. A dozen of these Spurs were shipped to the States, five to the Middle East and Europe and seven remained in the UK. The 25th car, and the actual 100,000th Rolls-Royce built, was kept by the company.

Despite the outward appearance that not a lot was happening, the engineering department was going through one of its busiest times without actually designing a new product. At the 1986 Paris Salon the

Above

Changes to the rear compartment are less dramatic, but note that all the doors now have elegant cross-banded cappings

Right

The latest Spirit's interior is much improved. Gone is the spindly steering wheel to be replaced by a leather one and the incongruous digital readouts by more traditional analogue instruments

fruits of that labour were revealed. Fuel injection was adopted across the range, anti-lock brakes were fitted to all models bar the Corniche and Phantom, and extensive interior improvements – including new electrically-operated seats – appeared. Changes were also made to the chassis to further improve ride and handling. But there was a tinge of sadness to all this progress. After 11 years the Camargue was discontinued. To mark the end of its distinguished career a dozen special cars were made exclusively for the American market. The Camargue's distinctive appearance was further enhanced by acrylic white paintwork and a white Everflex covered roof offset by twin scarlet coachlines. The headlamp surrounds were also finished in white and there was a Camargue Limited Edition badge on the boot. Tyres, Goodyear NCT 235/70 HR15s, were mounted on Rolls-Royce modified alloy rims. The special treatment continued inside with red Nuella hide piped in white with contrasting black carpets edged in red leather; even the steering

wheel was scarlet leather with white stitching. Fine silver lines were inlaid in the waist rails and door cappings together with the R-R monogram. To ensure a perfect fit the inlays were cut by laser. In-Car Entertainment (ICE) included a compact disc player, graphic equaliser and stereo radio/cassette player from Pioneer and a quartet of speakers. A cellular telephone with a 'hands-off' facility was also built into the central tunnel while rear seat passengers had a mini cocktail cabinet – complete with four crystal glasses and a pair of R-R monogrammed silver-plated hip flasks – built-in between the rear seats. As for the rear armrest itself that housed a silver vanity set comprising a long-handled mirror, hairbrush, comb and clothes brush, all silver plated and bearing the R-R monogram. Rolls-Royce also supplied a red hide attache case, complete with silver propelling pencil.

Mechanically, the car was to the latest US specification with the addition of an ultrasonic reversing aid and a sophisticated radio-operated alarm system. As a final touch the glovebox housed a special plaque recording that 'This Camargue Limited Edition is one of 12 special motor cars built to celebrate the 80th anniversary of a Rolls-Royce in the United States'. Each plaque also carried the number of the car in the series.

Production of the Phantom VI still continued at a very leisurely pace

Above
*To celebrate building its 100,000th car
in 1985, Rolls-Royce produced 25
special edition Silver Spurs*

Right
*Discreet badging on the boot told those
following that this was no ordinary Rolls-
Royce (see also overleaf)*

and just to confirm its place in the annals of motoring history the Worshipful Company of Coachbuilders and Coach Harnessmakers celebrated the centenary of the car in 1986 by awarding the Phantom VI with its Gold Certificate as 'the most elegant and pleasing production car, regardless of class or price'. A fitting tribute to a car that was nearing the end of its life – not for lack of orders, HM The Queen took delivery of a new PVI in 1987 – but because of growing safety legislation which deemed a number of the Phantom's external projections as unsafe. Nevertheless it was another five years before the final Phantom VI rolled out of Mulliner Park Ward's factory. It took 20 months to build the last Phantom VI – number 365 in the series – for Yorkshire businessman, George Moore. Even in the extraordinary terms of a Phantom, this was no ordinary car as he specified a 101-item 'want list' including walnut picnic table to fit over the front wings, detachable front and rear

Above left
Exterior badging of the Centenary Spur might have been modest, but the interior was a display of all of Crewe's finest traditions, with its cross-banded veneers and through-centre console

Left
Veneer panelling in the rear doors has a mirror-like finish. The door cappings are inlaid with silver and the intertwined Rs

Above
While between the front seats nestled the R-R monogrammed hipflasks and crystal tumblers

bumpers, silk curtains, two telephones, a barometer and altimeter, a fridge in the boot and an extra large cocktail cabinet. 'How much?' was a question which potential Phantom VI owners never asked, so what George Moore's cost is open to conjecture. But to give you some guidance a 'standard' PVI – if ever such a thing existed – was priced at £350,000.

The disappearance of the Phantom opened up a gap in the market for both Hoopers and Robert Jankel Design to exploit, especially in the Middle and Far East. While Hoopers has restricted itself to stretched and 'head of state' versions of Rolls-Royce saloons, RJD has been far more adventurous in its offerings to clients: as well as the lengthened cars, the Weybridge-based specialists produce convertible versions of the Spirit and, even, an estate version with part-time four-wheel drive. Although money and taste might not quite go hand-in-hand there is no disputing the level of craftsmanship employed. So, despite the traditional days of coachbuilding cars with unique bodies on separate chassis having passed, the idea of tailoring cars to a buyer's precise requirements hasn't and it's a niche which Rolls-Royce would, eventually, recognise and start to exploit itself. But before that happened the Silver Spirit needed bringing up to date. Rolls-Royce has always tended to be modest about its engineering achievements and, as we have read, followed rather than led

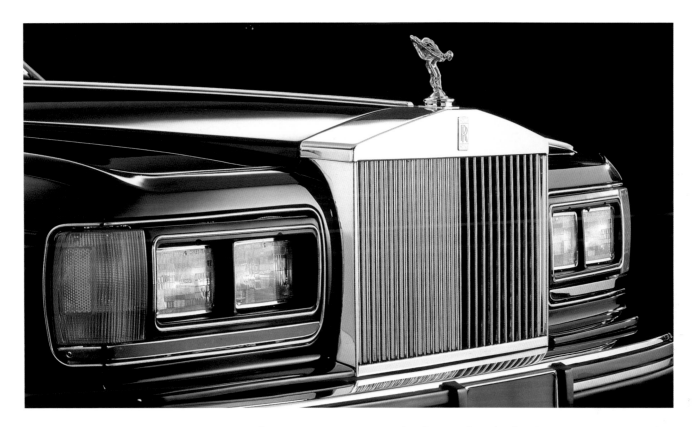

Above
*American specification models, such as
this Silver Spur II, were fitted with rather
ugly twin rectangular headlamps*

Left
*Because of production scheduling and
shipping demands it proved impossible to
get all 25 of the centenary Spurs
together at any one time. The nearest
Rolls-Royce got to was 21*

when it comes to new technology – discs brakes being a prime example.
That all changed in 1989 when the Silver Spirit and Spur II were
announced, complete with electronically-controlled adaptive damping.
Developed in-house by Rolls-Royce, the 'Automatic Ride Control' used
solenoid-operated Boge dampers which could be instantly switched to
one of three settings: soft, which is equal to a US specification Rolls-
Royce; normal, the equivalent of European standards; and firm, equal to
the Bentley Turbo R. A single 'black box' of micro-chips senses
longitudinal acceleration and deceleration as well as monitoring throttle
position, the brake pedal and steering angle. The system is completely
adaptive with soft as the default setting; above 70 mph it switches into
normal mode and beyond 100 mph into the firmest setting. In addition
new 6.5 ins rims were fitted on 15-spoke alloy wheels, though they were
covered with stainless steel trims. Interior refinements weren't as radical
as the suspensions;' a redesigned fascia with boxwood inlay and
'crossbanding' housed two large dials with an electronic warning lights
display separating them, and another pair of air vents. Those who
detested the thin-rimmed Bakelite steering wheel were delighted to note

that it had been replaced by a thicker, two-spoke, leather-rimmed tiller. These improvements – apart from the ARC system – were also read across to the Corniche convertible which eventually got the intelligent suspension system. Rolls-Royce therefore entered the 1990s with a range of cars – though now getting rather long in the tooth by industry standards – brim full of current technology.

But the start of the new decade was as cruel to Rolls-Royce as the early eighties had been: recession and falling sales forced huge cutbacks in production and, consequently, staff. In 1991 Mulliner Park Ward was closed and Corniche production transferred in its entirety to Crewe, which had plenty of spare capacity. On a more positive note, the Rolls-Royce Touring Limousine was unveiled at that year's Frankfurt Motor Show. Essentially it was Crewe's answer to the stretched cars which Hooper and RJD had been successfully selling for the past six years or so. Based on the Silver Spur II saloon, the Mulliner Park Ward-badged limousine measured 235 ins bumper to bumper, a 24 ins increase over the Spur, and was 573 lbs heavier. The roofline was increased for improved interior headroom and there were deeper rear quarter panels

Right
The latter part of the '80s had seen a boom in coachbuilt conversions by the likes of RJD and Hoopers. This 1990 Silver Spur II used the Mulliner Park Ward moniker to indicate that it was more than just a Bordeaux-painted Spur with colour-keyed bumpers and stainless steel mouldings to the door sills and wheel arches

Above
The Silver Spur II received the same mechanical improvements as the Spirit in 1990

and a smaller rear window. The car's stately opulence continued inside where virtually all the two-foot increase in length was devoted to the rear comfort of passengers. An electrically-operated division, with a privacy blind, was installed immediately behind the front pair of seats and there were also a pair of fully-trimmed occasional seats as well as a fully equipped cocktail cabinet and audio visual cabinet complete with a stacker CD system. The list went on and on so that the Touring Limousine continued the high standards established by the Phantom while optional extras even included a telefax machine, although the glass moonroof with its electrically-powered screen was standard. Rolls-Royce planned to produce just 25 of these cars a year.

With the intervals between model replacements being so long it is hardly surprising that Rolls-Royce tend to celebrate more birthdays than many other manufacturers, and so it was in October 1992, when the 'Anniversary' edition of the Corniche was unveiled at the Paris Salon some 21 years after the car first appeared. From the outside these Ming Blue cars – of which only 25 were built – don't look that different. Sure there are special body badges, stainless steel wheel arch and door sill embellishers as well as unique wheel trim motifs but that is all. But once you start to look round the Magnolia hide interior it doesn't take long to appreciate Crewe's craftsmanship and artistry: uniquely patterned burr

Above
An American-specification Corniche III with stainless steel embellishers to the wheel arches

Above right
A UK market Corniche III with colour-keyed bumpers and door mirrors

Right
With a basic design that is now nudging 20 years old, the Spur is beginning to look a little dated – especially at the front with the large oblong headlamp and indicator units

elm veneer with oak crossbanding and silver inlays are standard. There are handcrafted silver inlays and R-R motifs in the door capping rails and picnic tables and an engraved plaque in the veneered glove box to identify that this is one of 25 special cars. With its lustrous blue paintwork and cream hood the 'Anniversary' Corniche is a fitting tribute to a car whose elegance has withstood the test of time and established it as an all-time classic.

As Rolls-Royce prepares itself for a new millennium it faces its toughest challenge to date. A changing world with new values is forcing the Crewe management to make a radical rethink of how Rolls-Royce will cope in a future where fuel efficiency and emissions will become increasingly important. It is unthinkable that Rolls-Royce won't be building cars when that new century dawns, or that Rolls-Royce won't be celebrating its centenary a few years later. Just what those cars will be like is something not even the industry's soothsayers can prophesy, but one thing is certain: future Rolls-Royce cars will always be a supreme excellence.

Above
The USA, with its love of chauffeur-driven limousines, has always been a strong market for the Spur

Above right
This picture clearly depicts the Spur's extra-long rear door. Rear passengers also have the luxury of veneered picnic tables and individually reclining seat backs

Right
Many Spurs are chauffeur-driven, but unlike the Phantom, where the driver definitely comes off second best, the Spur's driver is well cared for

Above

Despite its American-style front number plate this Spur will be delivered to a Middle Eastern customer

Left

A 1993 Spur destined for the North American market

The latest intrpretation of a classic theme. The Corniche IV might look similar to the car launched in 1971, but beneath the skin it is a very different animal

Above
One of just 25 Anniversary Corniches built to celebrate 21 years of a classic design

Opposite
The cubby holes house cocktail requisites and a set of leather-bound notepads, etc

Above
Inside the Touring Limousine is just what you'd expect of a car wearing the Mulliner Park Ward badge – exquisite detailing and sumptuous fittings

Right
Rolls-Royce launched its own stretched Spur in 1992. The Touring Limousine, however, also has its roof height increased which helps to balance the increase in overall length

Coachbuilt specials

Tailor-made motoring is back in fashion, even if some of the styling and taste is rather distinctive.

Coach building as a craft virtually died with the Phantom VI, in fact only Aston Martin and the like continue the tradition of hand-forming panels for low-volume production cars.

While it is easy to blame rising costs and the lack of demand for bespoke motoring, the real culprit behind the demise of coachbuilt cars is legislation. Faceless bureaucrats the world over demand more and more tests to prove cars are safer, protecting passengers and pedestrians equally. It is no longer financially viable for manufacturers to keep crash-testing cars which might never reach four-figure production runs.

That's the real reason why there was never a successor to the Phantom VI or the Camargue.

But in the 1980s all that started to change. Suddenly the new-found wealth of the Middle and Far East based on oil and electronics wanted an outlet for display: exotic properties, magnificent yachts, sumptuous 'planes to jet their owners round the world and distinctive limousines waiting at their beck and call were de rigeur.

If manufacturers couldn't meet their needs because of the Type Approval regulations then others would, which is where the likes of RJD and Hoopers come into the equation.

While manufacturers might be banned from converting cars, there is nothing in the Type Approval regulations to prevent a private individual from doing so – especially if that individual happens to own or run the country involved.

Basically, what companies like RJD and Hoopers do is to convert a customer's existing car; in other words the customer buys and registers the car and then hands it over to the coach builder. Having said that, neither of the two operations mentioned are crude 'cut and shut' merchants; RJD, for instance won a contract from Rolls-Royce in the early Eighties to produce a run of stretched limousines based on the Spur. Since then the company has forged an enviable reputation for the quality of workmanship and body engineering which is equal to anything produced by the factory.

Whilst Rolls-Royce casts a disapproving eye over much of RJD and Hoopers work – one suspects more because of the clients' sense of style rather than anything else – one cannot deny that both organisations

Rolls-Royce has always tried to meet customer demands. But as the 1980s progressed, customers wanted their cars more personalised than ever before. There is now a special department at Crewe dedicated to meeting customer requests, whether that is the simplicity of a sophisticated stereo system, a writing table in the back of a Spur for example, or veneer panelling and storage pockets for bottles and glasses (right)

In recent years companies like Hoopers have built some truly extravagant conversions based on current Rolls-Royce models. Established in 1807, Hoopers were coachbuilders to Queen Victoria and to King Edward for nearly 50 years. The association with Rolls-Royce started in 1909. The Emperor State Limousine is based on a Silver Spirit with 8.5 ins added to the front doors, 8 ins to the rear doors and 23.5 ins to the rear quarter panel. The roof line has been raised 3.5 ins and the door height two inches. Weighing 5764 lbs unladen the 247.4 ins long car will seat five passengers in the rear compartment where there is the usual array of cocktail cabinet, video and Hi-Fi centre etc. (Photos courtesy of Hoopers)

satisfied a demand. It now seems that Rolls-Royce has, belatedly, recognised this and has resuscitated the Mulliner Park Ward badge in an attempt to meet the demands of those Rolls-Royce owners who want a car tailored to their unique specifications.

As yet Crewe hasn't started converting pre-registered cars, but as its

If there is one firm of independents which has established itself as pre-eminent in the field of Rolls-Royce conversions it is Robert Jankel Design. Relatively young by Hooper's standards, Jankel was established in 1960, and since then has produced many prototypes for mainstream manufacturers as well as building the stretched Spur Limousine for Rolls-Royce. The Weybridge-based company will undertake almost any project for clients around the world, as well as a 'standard' model range. Though the cars themselves are anything but standard. The Azur Spyder is a four-seater convertible version of the Silver Spirit saloon with a fully automatic, self-locking and power-operated hood. Interior dimensions are identical to the saloon it is based on. (Photos courtesy of RJD)

marketing men talk more and more about "finely focused" cars appealing to a "very discerning clientele of, perhaps, one" you're left with the distinct impression that coachbulit specials might be about to return. And at a time when cars are becoming less distinctive, that surely can't be a bad thing.

Above

One of Jankel's more bizarre creations is a four-wheel drive estate model. The Val d'Isere has an estate back with a fifth-door grafted on and comes with an optional four-wheel drive system, developed by Jankel. The front wheels are driven hydraulically by motors built into modified front hub assemblies. Drive to the front wheels is engaged by selecting low or reverse gear and is automatically disengaged once vehicle speed exceeds 30 mph. (Photo courtesy of RJD)

Opposite

The Antibes features a modest 10 ins stretch to the rear quarter panels. As a result rear passengers benefit from a console containing colour television and video, audio system, slide-out writing tables, a refrigerator and a secondary airconditioning system. A glass division is also installed. (Photos courtesy of RJD)

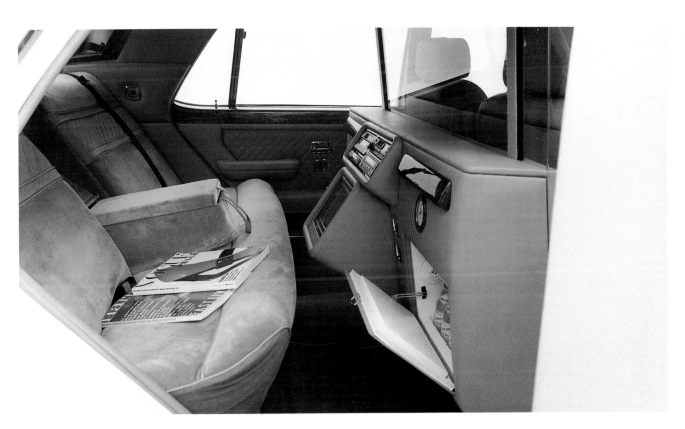

Insert 42 ins into a Spirit's wheelbase and you get the Nice limousine, similar in appearance and style to the conversion Jankel did for Rolls-Royce. An unusual feature of Jankel's conversions is the use of exotic timber; this one uses Black Ebony. (Photos courtesy of RJD)

There is no set formula to Jankel's range of options as can be seen from these photographs of a Spur II with a 44 inch stretch. Exterior paintwork can be specified to a customer's particular demands, while the interior layout can be made to measure. (Photos courtesy of RJD)

Above

The Royale predated Rolls-Royce's own Touring Limousine as a replacement for the Phantom VI and competes with Hoopers similar conversion. The rear quarter of the car and rear doors are extended by 46 ins, the door height by two inches and the roof by a further four inches. Naturally, there is a division between the front and rear compartments and one unique touch is that the rearward-facing seats – which are to the same dimensions as the standard rear seats – can be removed for even more leg room. (Photo courtesy of RJD)

Opposite

One Far Eastern customer demanded an extra 71 ins to be grafted into his limousine so it would be longer than a rival's. And, yes, that really is a veneered table in the rear compartment. (Photos courtesy of RJD)

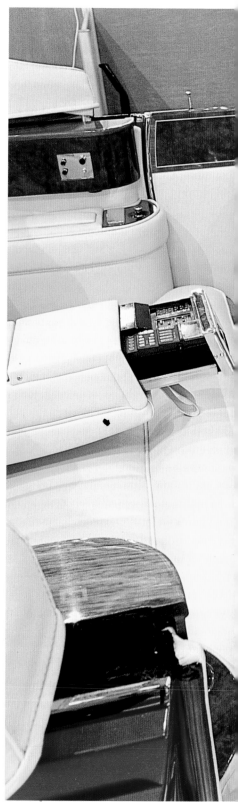

Above

Perhaps not the prettiest Rolls-Royce Phantom VI ever built, but certainly the most extravagant. This is one of two chassis supplied to the Italian coachbuilder, Frua in the early 1970s. One car was completed and displayed at the Frankfurt Motor Show in 1973, before Frua's death. After he died the second car lay unfinished in a lock-up until some wealthy enthusiasts found it and sponsored its completion, unveiling this unique car at the 1993 Geneva Salon. (Photo: Peter Robain)

Right

The interior is as luxurious and extravagant as any car ever built. Just who would want to buy it remained open to conjecture when the car was debuted, especially as the rumoured asking price was in the region of £2 million. (Photo: Peter Robain)

Technical specifications

ROLLS-ROYCE SILVER CLOUD II & III

[ ] = [Long-wheelbase models]

Engine
Cylinders: V8
Fuel supply: Twin SU HD6 1.75 ins carburetters (Twin SU HD8 2 ins carburetters)
Bore/Stroke (mm): 104.1/91.4
Cubic capacity (cc): 6230
Compression ratio: 8.0:1 (9.0:1)
Valve gear: In-line ohv
Ignition: Delco double contact breaker with single coil
Main bearings: 5

Transmission
Rolls-Royce/GM four-speed automatic
Overall gear ratios
1st: 3.08
2nd: 4.47
3rd: 8.10
4th: 11.77
Reverse: 13.24:1
Rear axle: 3.08:1
Top gear ratio: 27.3 mph/1000 rpm

Wheels and Tyres
8.20-15 tubeless tyres on 6 ins 5 stud steel wheels
Brakes: F/R: 11.25 ins dia x 3 ins drums
Steering: Power-assisted cam-and-roller
Lock-to-lock: 4.5 turns
Turning circle: 41.75 ft
Measurements (ins)
Length: 212 [216]
Width: 74.5
Height: 64.25
Wheelbase: 123
Track (F/R): 58.5/60
Ground clearance: 7 ins
Kerb weight (lbs): 4452

Suspension
Front: Independent by coil springs, unequal length wishbones, anti-roll bar and hydraulic dampers
Rear: Live axle with half-elliptic leaf springs, adjustable lever-arm hydraulic dampers and 'Z-bar'

Performance figures (mph/secs)
Silver Cloud II Silver Cloud III
0-60 11.5 10.8
0-100 38.5 34.2
1/4 mile 18.2 17.7
Max speed (mph) 113 116
Average mpg 11.8 12.3

Production figures
2716 2297

ROLLS-ROYCE SILVER SHADOW I, (II), [WRAITH I], {WRAITH II}

Engine
Cylinders: V8
Fuel supply: Twin SU HD8 2 ins carburetters ({Twin SU HIF7 carburetters}). Bosch K-Jetronic fuel-injection for California only from 1980 onwards
Bore/stroke (mm): 104.1 x 91.4. 104.1 x 99.1 from 1970 onwards
Compression ratio: 9.0:1 8.0:1 or 7.3:1 <USA specification> from 1975 onwards
Valve gear: In-line ohv
Ignition: Delco double contact breaker with single coil. 1975, OPUS electronic ignition
Main bearings: 5

Transmission
Rolls-Royce/GM four-speed automatic, right-hand drive only. GM300, three-speed automatic for left-hand drive export models and all Silver Wraiths
4-speed 3-speed
1st: 3.08 3.08
2nd: 4.466 4.558
3rd: 8.10 7.638
4th: 11.77
Reverse: 13.24 6.406
Rear axle: 3.08 3.08
Top gear ratio: 26.2 mph/1000 rpm 70 MPH = 2670 RPM
Wheels and Tyres
8.45 – 15 ins cross-ply tyres on 6 ins rimmed steel wheels
From 1972, all cars fitted with radial 205VR15 ins.
From 1974, all cars fitted with 235/70 ins or HR70HR15 ins radials

Brakes
Front/rear: 11 ins discs all round with three separate high pressure hydraulic circuits

Steering
Power-assisted recirculating-ball. ({1977, Power-assisted rack-and-pinion})
Turns lock-to-lock: 4.25 ({3.5})
Turning circle (ft): 35.5 between kerbs (39{40.4})Measurements (ins)
Shadow I LWB Shadow II Wraith II
Length: 203.5 207.5 204.5 207.5/208.5
Width: 71 71.7
Height: 59.75
Wheelbase: 119.5 123.5 120 124
Front track: 57.5 60 <'74 on>
b 57.5 59.6 <'74 on>
Ground clearance: 6.5
Kerb weight (lbs): 4659 5010 4930 5010 – 5260

Suspension
Front: Independent, coil springs, wishbones, telescopic dampers, anti-roll bar. Automatic hydraulic height control
Rear: Independent, coil springs, single trailing arms, telescopic dampers. Automatic hydraulic height control

Performance figures (secs)
Shadow I Shadow II Wraith II
6230 cc/6750 cc
0-60mph: 10.9/10.2 13.7 10.1
0-100mph: 37.8/33.6 N/AVAILABLE 32.4
1/4 mile: 17.6/17.5 N/A 17.3
Max mph: 115/117 117 119
Average mpg: 12.2/12.4 N/A 13.2
Production figures
16,717 + 2776 long-wheelbase 8422 2144

ROLLS-ROYCE CAMARGUE

Engine
Cylinders: V8
Fuel supply: Twin SU HD8 2 ins carburetters for first 31 cars. Then four-choke Solex 4A1 carburetter for all markets bar USA, Japan, Australia etc. 1980; Bosch K-Jetronic fuel injection for Californian cars and for all USA/Japanese cars from 1981 onwards
Bore/stroke (mm): 104.1 x 91.4. 104.1 x 99.1 from 1970 onwards
Compression ratio: 8.0:1 or 7.3:1 USA specification
Valve gear: In-line ohv
Ignition: Delco double contact breaker with single coil. 1975, OPUS electronic ignition
Main bearings: 5

Transmission
Rolls-Royce/GM four-speed automatic. 1970, GM400 three-speed
4-speed 3-speed
1st: 3.08 3.08
2nd: 4.466 4.558
3rd: 8.10 7.638
4th: 11.77 -
Reverse: 13.24 6.406
Rear axle: 3.08 3.08
Top gear ratio: 26.2 mph/1000 rpm

Wheels and Tyres
Wheels: 15X6 ins
Tyres: 235/70HR 15 ins radials

Brakes
Front/rear: 11 ins discs (ventilated at front) all round with three separate high pressure hydraulic circuits

Steering
Power-assisted recirculating-ball. 1977, Power-assisted rack-and-pinion
Turns lock-to-lock: 4.25/3.5
Turning circle (ft): 39.0 between kerbs

Measurements (ins)
Length: 203.5
Width: 75.5
Height: 56
Wheelbase: 120
Track (F/R): 60.0/59.6
Ground clearance: N/AVAILABLE
Kerb weight (lbs): 5175

Suspension
Front: Independent, coil springs, wishbones, telescopic dampers, anti-roll bar. Automatic hydraulic height control
Rear: Independent, coil springs, single trailing arms, telescopic dampers. Automatic hydraulic height control

Max mph: 120
Average mpg: N/A

Production figures
534, including four prototypes without chassis numbers plus a quartet of experimental cars which were scrapped. Actual number sold 526

ROLLS-ROYCE SILVER SPIRIT/(SPUR 1), & [SILVER SPIRIT]/ {SPUR II}

Engine
Fuel supply: Twin SU HIF7 carburetters. 1980, Bosch K-Jetronic fuel injection for California models and from 1987 Bosch K-Motronic on all cars
Bore/Stroke (mm): 104.1/99.1
Cubic capacity (cc): 6750
Compression ratio: 9.0:1, 8.0:1
Valve gear: In-line ohv
Ignition: Delco double contact breaker with single coil
Main bearings: 5

Transmission
Rolls-Royce/GM four-speed automatic. GM400 three-speed automatic. [{GM Hydramatic 4L80-E}]
Overall gear ratios
1st: 3.08, 2.50
2nd: 4.47, 1.50
3rd: 8.10, 1.00
4th: 11.77
Reverse: 13.24:1, N/A
Rear axle: 3.08:1, 2.69:1, [{3.07:1}]
Top gear ratio: 27.3 mph/1000 rpm, 26.3 mph/1000 rpm, N/A

Wheels and Tyres
235/70/HR15 6.5 ins steel wheels [{6.5J 15 light alloy 235/70 R 15 V}]

Brakes
F/R: 11.06 ins dia ventilated discs/10.9 ins dia solid discs [{ABS}]

Steering
Power-assisted recirculating ball. [{Power-assisted rack-and-pinion}]
Lock-to-lock: 4.25 turns. [{3.25 turns}]
Turning circle (ft): 41.75 (40.3) [39.5] {41.0}

Measurements (ins)
Length: 207.4 {211.4}
Width: 74.3
Height: 58.5
Wheelbase: 120.5 {124.5}
Track (F/R): 60.5/60.5
Ground clearance: 5.3
Kerb weight (lbs): 4949 (5059) [5180] {5247}

Suspension
Front: Independent by coil springs with lower wishbones, compliant controlled upper levers, telescopic dampers and anti-roll bar mounted on the front sub frame. [{ Automatic Ride Control}]
Rear: Independent coil spring arrangement with semi-trailing arms, suspension struts, gas springs and anti-roll bar. [{Automatic Ride Control}]

Performance figures (mph/secs)
Spirit II
0-60 10.4
0-100 32.9
1/4 mile 17.4
Max speed (mph) 123
Average mpg 14.4

Production figures (end of March, 1993)
8476 6394 N/A N/A

ROLLS-ROYCE SILVER SPUR LIMOUSINE & (SPUR II TOURING LIMOUSINE)

Engine
Cylinders: V8
Fuel supply: Twin SU HIF7 carburetters. 1987, Bosch K-Motronic fuel injection for all models
Bore/Stroke (mm): 104.1/99.1
Cubic capacity (cc): 6750
Compression ratio: 9.0:1, 8.0:1
Valve gear: In-line ohv
Ignition: Delco double contact breaker with single coil.
Main bearings: 5

Transmission
GM400 three-speed automatic. (GM Hydramatic 4L80-E)
Overall gear ratios
1st: 2.50,
2nd: 1.50,
3rd: 1.00,
4th: 0.75
Reverse: N/A
Rear axle: 2.69:1, (3.07:1)
Top gear ratio: 30/35 mph / 1000 rpm

Wheels and Tyres
235/70/HR15 6.5 ins steel wheels (6.5 J 15 light alloy 235/70 R 15 V)

Brakes
F/R: 11.06 ins dia ventilated discs/10.9ins dia solid discs (ABS)

Steering
Power-assisted recirculating ball. (Power-assisted rack-and-pinion)
Lock-to-lock: 4.25 turns. (3.25 turns)
Turning circle (ft): N/A 44.3

Measurements (ins)
Length: 243.4 (235.4)
Width: 74.3
Height: 58.5 (60.4)
Wheelbase: 156.5 (148.5)
Track (F/R): 60.5/60.5
Ground clearance: 5.3
Kerb weight (lbs): N/A (5820)

Suspension
Front: Independent by coil springs with lower wishbones, compliant controlled upper levers, telescopic dampers and anti-roll bar mounted on the front sub frame. (Automatic Ride Control)
Rear: Independent coil spring arrangement with semi-trailing arms, suspension struts, gas springs and anti-roll bar. (Automatic Ride Control)

ROLLS-ROYCE SILVER SHADOW TWO-DOOR CONVERTIBLE & (SALOON)

Engine
Cylinders: V8
Fuel supply: Twin SU HD8 2 ins carburetters
Capacity (cc): 6250/6750
Bore/stroke (mm): 104.1 x 91.4/104.1 x 99.1
Compression ratio: 9.0:1
Valve gear: In-line ohv
Ignition: Delco double contact breaker with single coil
Main bearings: 5

Transmission
Rolls-Royce/GM four-speed automatic, right-hand drive only. GM300, three-speed automatic for left-hand drive export models
4-speed 3-speed
1st: 3.08 3.08
2nd: 4.466 4.558
3rd: 8.10 7.638
4th: 11.77
Reverse: 13.24 6.406
Rear axle: 3.08 3.08
Top gear ratio: 26.2 mph/1000 rpm

Wheels and Tyres
8.45 – 15 ins cross-ply tyres on 6 ins rimmed steel wheels.

Brakes
Front/rear: 11 ins discs all round with three separate high pressure hydraulic circuits
Steering
Power-assisted recirculating-ball
Turns lock-to-lock: 4.25
Turning circle (ft): 38 between kerbs

Measurements (ins)
Length: 203.5
Width: 72.0
Height: 59.75 (58.75)
Wheelbase: 19.5
Track (F/R): 57.5
Ground clearance: 6.5
Kerb weight (lbs): 5124 (4978)

Suspension
Front: Independent, coil springs, wishbones, telescopic dampers, anti-roll bar. Automatic hydraulic height control
Rear: Independent, coil springs, single trailing arms, telescopic dampers. Automatic hydraulic height control

Performance figures (secs)*
Convertible Saloon
6230 cc/6750 cc 6230 cc/6750 cc
0-60 mph: N/A 9.6
0-100 mph: N/A 30.0
1/4 mile: 17.1
Max mph: 120
Average mpg: 11.9

Production figures
504 607

ROLLS-ROYCE CORNICHE (S1) {S11} [S111] <S1V>

Engine
Cylinders: V8
Fuel supply: Twin SU HD8 2 ins carburetters. Then four-choke Solex 4A1 carburetter for all markets bar USA, Japan, Australia etc. 1981 Bosch K-Jetronic fuel injection for all USA/Japanese cars and from 1987 onwards Bosch K-Motronic for all markets
Capacity (cc): 6250/6750
Bore/stroke (mm): 104.1 x 91.4 104.1 x 99.1
Compression ratio: 9.0:1 [<8.0:1>]
Valve gear: In-line ohv
Ignition: Delco double contact breaker with single coil
Main bearings: 5

Transmission
GM400, three-speed automatic <GM Hydramatic 4L80-E>
3-speed 4-speed
1st: 3.08 2.50 2.48
2nd: 4.558 1.50 1.48
3rd: 7.638 1.00 1.00
4th: – 0.75
Reverse: 6.406 N/A
Rear axle: 3.08 3.07

Wheels and Tyres
(8.45 – 15 ins cross-ply tyres on 6 ins rimmed steel wheels. Then 205VR15 radial tyres and later 235/70HR15). {235/70HR15}. [235/70HR15]. <6.5 ins J 15 light alloy wheels, 235/70R 15V tyres>

Brakes
Front/rear: 11 ins discs all round with three separate high pressure hydraulic circuits <ABS>

Steering
Power-assisted recirculating-ball [<Power-assisted rack-and-pinion>]
Turns lock-to-lock: 4.25 [<3.25>]
Turning circle (ft): 39.0 between kerbs [<39.5>]

Measurements (ins)
Length: (203.5) {[<204.5>]}
Width: 72.0
Height: 59.75
Wheelbase: 119.5 [<120.5>]
Track (F/R): 57.5
Ground clearance: 6.5
Kerb weight (lbs): 5124 (4978)

Suspension
Front: Independent, coil springs, wishbones, telescopic dampers, anti-roll bar. Automatic hydraulic height control. <Automatic Ride Control>
Rear: Independent, coil springs, single trailing arms, telescopic dampers. Automatic hydraulic height control. <Automatic Ride Control>

Average mpg: 120/126/128

Production figures
2013# 1905## N/A
#Includes 780 saloons ##Includes 310 saloons

ROLLS-ROYCE PHANTOM V AND (VI)

Engine
Cylinders: V8
Fuel supply: Twin SU HD8 2 ins carburetters (Twin SU HIF7 carburetters)
Bore/Stroke (mm): 104.1/91.4 (104.1/99.1)
Cubic capacity (cc): 6230 (6750)
Compression ratio: 8.0:1 (9.0:1)
Valve gear: In-line ohv
Ignition: Delco double contact breaker with single coil
Main bearings: 5

Transmission
Rolls-Royce/GM four-speed automatic (GM 400 three-speed automatic)
Overall gear ratios
1st: 3.89 (3.89)
2nd: 5.64 (5.757)
3rd: 10.23 (9.647)
4th: 14.86
Reverse: 16.72 (8.091)
Rear axle: 3.89:1
Top gear ratio: 22.5 mph/1000 rpm (22.5 mph/1000 rpm)

Wheels and Tyres
8.90-15 tubeless tyres on 6 ins steel wheels

Brakes
F/R: 11.25 ins dia x 3 ins drums

Steering
Power-assisted cam-and-roller
Lock-to-lock: 4.25 turns
Turning circle: 48.00 ft

Measurements (ins) all dimensions might vary slightly according to bodywork fitted
Length: 238
Width: 79.0
Height: 69.0
Wheelbase: 145
Track (F/R): 60.9/64
Ground clearance: 7.75
Kerb weight (lbs): 5600 (6000)

Suspension
Front: Independent by coil springs, wishbones, anti-roll bar and lever arm hydraulic dampers
Rear: Live axle with half-elliptic leaf springs, adjustable lever-arm hydraulic dampers

Performance figures (mph/secs)
0-60 13.8 N/A
0-100 N/A
1/4 mile 19.4 N/A
Max speed (mph) 101.2 N/A
Average mpg 11.1 N/A

Production figures
793 365